Liberating Belsen

*Remembering the Soldiers of the
Durham Light Infantry*

— DAVID LOWTHER —

Sacristy Press
PO Box 612, Durham, DH1 9HT

www.sacristy.co.uk

First published in 2015 by Sacristy Press, Durham

Sacristy Limited, registered in England & Wales, number 7565667

British Library Cataloguing-in-Publication Data
A catalogue record for the book is available from the British Library

ISBN 978-1-908381-91-0

CONTENTS

PHOTOGRAPHS

LIST OF MAPS

Figure 1: Regimental badge of the Durham Light
Infantry (illustration: Kenneth Crawford).

INTRODUCTION

This book is about a small group of soldiers, some of whom were conscripted to fight in the Second World War while others were either career or territorial (part-time) troops. All received solid training in the requirements of war although, in common with most of Britain's land forces, they were underprepared at the start of the conflict. Some of them had seen action in different parts of the world and had faced danger, seen comrades die, retreated and, later, chased the retreating enemy. Nothing, no amount of training, could have prepared them for what some of them discovered on 18 April 1945, less than a month before the end of the war in Europe.

The Second World War began on 1 September 1939, when German forces invaded Poland. It ended just a day over six years later, on 2 September 1945, when the Empire of Japan signed a document of surrender on board United States Ship Missouri, although Japanese forces had ceased fighting on 14 August.

The war was split into two parts: the war in Europe which lasted from September 1939 until May 1945 and the war in the Far East which began with the Japanese attack on the base of the United States Pacific Fleet at Pearl Harbour in the Hawaiian Islands on 7 December 1941. The war in the Far East ended in September 1945. Although there were two separate wars, the Germans, Italians and Japanese (known as the Axis powers) were allies, as were Great Britain, the Soviet Union and the United States. The Soviet Union didn't declare war on Japan until 9 August 1945 because they had already suffered terrible losses in the final attack on Germany. So although a case could be made that there were two wars, both were so intricately linked that the two have, rightly, always been treated as one.

The Second World War was one of the most catastrophic events in recent human history. Other wars have lasted longer: the Hundred Years War between France and England between 1337 and 1453 for example. The Thirty Years War (1618–1648) resulted in approximately one-third of the citizens of what we now call Germany dying either in battle or from disease or famine. Just twenty years before the outbreak of the Second World War, the Great War (which we now call the First World War) had ended with around ten million soldiers, sailors and airmen losing their lives along with seven million civilians.

All of these events are totally overshadowed by the staggering statistics for the Second World War in which approximately fifty-five million people died. That's about the same number as the population of England in 2014. The biggest casualty rates were in the Soviet Union (including present-day Russia, Belarus and Ukraine) where twenty million people lost their lives. Fifteen million Chinese died fighting the Japanese. Germany lost five million, Poland three million and the Japanese two and a half million. Britain lost three hundred and sixty thousand in conflict and sixty thousand in air raids. Three hundred thousand US fighting men were killed in action.

Compare these horrifying numbers with the wars of today, Afghanistan for instance, where the total number of the dead is less than three and a half thousand. This total includes just under four hundred and fifty armed forces personnel from Great Britain.

The sheer scale of the Second World War does indeed dwarf all other conflicts. Many died on battlefields, others in the air and thousands at sea. Civilians all over the world perished in air raids and even more from disease and famine. These were the tragic casualties of war. However, of those fifty five million, over six million, a little over ten per cent, were murdered. A majority of these were Jewish, although there were a significant number of political deaths, killings of innocent civilians and minorities. This book is about how the world came to hear about these murders in what later came to be called the Holocaust—the collective extermination of almost six million Jewish men, women and children. It is also about the men who uncovered those monstrous crimes in 1945 and the traumatic effect it had on their lives. You will read the words of some of those men who made the ghastly discoveries and the thoughts of some of the survivors of the Bergen-Belsen concentration camp.

In this book, I shall sketch in a brief history of the Durham Light Infantry (Chapter One), follow their campaigns in the Second World War (Chapter Two) and detail the history of the German concentration camp system and outcome of what the Nazis called the *final solution of the Jewish question* (Chapter Three). Chapter Four will tell the story of the Bergen-Belsen camp and Chapter Five will follow the soldiers from the beaches of Normandy to the gates of Belsen. Chapter Six will deal with the liberation of the camp in 1945 and Chapter Seven will tell of the aftermath for the survivors, the liberators, the soldiers, the guards and their superiors who held men, women and children captive in the camp in the most atrocious conditions.

I shall not use detailed notes on each page but will acknowledge every source, be it written, on film and photograph, or on audio tape, in a chapter at the end of the book. Some readers may be interested to know how the war broke out. The simple answer is that the aggressors, Germany and Japan, attacked peaceful nations, Poland and the United States of America, without provocation. The complete answer is, of course, far more complicated and so, for those interested in finding out about the causes of the war, I have pointed out possible directions for further research.

Why should there be yet another book on the Second World War? This book is targeted at young people who may be unfamiliar with some of the details of those dreadful times in the middle years of the twentieth century. I hope that they will feel pride in the contributions that their grandparents and great-grandparents made in ensuring that the Allies triumphed in a war that had to be fought and had to be won. Had the British Prime Minister Neville Chamberlain not declared war on Germany on 3 September 1939, Hitler, and later Mussolini, would have had a free hand in their aggressive foreign policy and the outcome of the Second World War may well have been different. And then, finally, never forget the six million who died in the Holocaust. If we forget, it may happen again.

CHAPTER ONE

INFANTRYMEN
The Story of the Durham Light Infantry 1758-1968

Soldiers are citizens of death's grey land.
Siegfried Sassoon, 1918

The Durham Light Infantry, one of the best known and toughest regiments of both the First and Second World Wars, began life as the 68th Regiment of Foot. It was raised in 1758 by a Durham man, Lieutenant-Colonel John Lambton of the Coldstream Guards. Lambton was also an MP and represented Durham City in parliament for many years. Long before the days of army recruiting offices, officials of various regiments went through towns, villages and cities recruiting soldiers, many of whom "signed up" knowing that this was the best way, and in some cases the only way, of earning a living. Although Lambton was from County Durham, the first 68th Foot was drawn from many parts of the country. It was, as the name suggests, a regiment of infantry or foot soldiers as opposed to troops on horseback who were known as cavalry.

Dressed in the famous British Army redcoats, the 68th first saw action during the Seven Years War, an almost global conflict in which the main players were Great Britain on one side and France on the other. These two countries, along with Spain later in the war, were, at that time, the world's leading empire builders who had seized land in all corners of the globe. Clashes over colonial ambitions and trade were the chief causes of this war which lasted from 1756 to 1763.

By 1782, the regiment became most closely associated with County Durham, with many of its soldiers coming from that part of North East England. Shortly after this, a series of conflicts broke out between Great Britain and France. The French had ridden themselves of their king and queen during the early part of the French Revolution (1789) and both were beheaded at the guillotine. From the chaos of post-revolutionary France, there emerged a leader of outstanding ability and great ambition, Napoléon Bonaparte. Britain and her allies fought Napoléon's armies and ships on and off for more than twenty years, ending with Napoléon's defeat at the Battle of Waterloo in 1815.

It was during one part of this war, the Peninsular War, that the 68th first gained a reputation as great warriors. The Peninsular War was fought in Spain and Portugal between 1807 and 1814. Napoléon was trying to seize Spain and add her to his empire. The British, under their commander Sir Arthur Wellesley (later the Duke of Wellington and victor over Napoléon at Waterloo) were trying to stop this from happening. The 68th Foot fought with great distinction and established themselves as a regiment to be reckoned with in the British Army.

We next hear of the 68th Foot in the Crimean War (1853–1856). This time the British and French fought on the same side, along with the Turks. The Turkish Empire (called the Ottoman Empire) was falling apart and the Russians, keen to expand their own Empire, thought they'd seize some of it for themselves. This war is best remembered for the great nurse Florence Nightingale, the suicidal Charge of the Light Brigade at the Battle of Balaclava, and the introduction of the Victoria Cross which, was the highest award for gallantry that Britain made to her soldiers and sailors (and, later, airmen). Two of the first to be given this great honour were from the 68th Foot. An Irishman, Private John Byrne, earned his VC after a ferocious bayonet duel with a Russian soldier at the Battle of Inkerman in 1854 and Captain Thomas de Courcy Hamilton, a Scotsman, was honoured after a desperate defence against the counter-attacking Russians at the siege of Sebastopol the following year.

During this bloody war, the 68th Foot covered themselves in glory and played an important part in the Battle of Alma as well as Sebastopol and Inkerman. The Crimean War ended with the Franco-British and Turkish Alliance defeating the Russians whose territorial ambitions were halted by the Peace of Paris in 1856.

Figure 2: Men of the 68th (Durham) Regiment of Foot (Light Infantry) in ordinary dress, during the Crimean War.

Almost every war that was fought between the end of the sixteenth century and the close of the Second World War was about territory. Earlier wars had often been about religion. The British, French, Spanish and Ottoman Empires were later joined by Prussia (later to become the German empire) in the last quarter of the nineteenth century and, later still, the Japanese Empire. The most common cause of these conflicts was usually who controlled which piece of land and who could seize the minerals and foodstuffs from these countries. Britain was trying to control her ever growing Empire but sometimes the natives of these conquered countries themselves rose up and tried to remove whichever imperial power was trying to occupy their territory. So it was that the next time the 68th Foot found itself in action was in New Zealand (1864) where the local population, the Maoris, fought, unsuccessfully, against the imperial power, the British. Again they battled with great determination and another Victoria Cross was won.

In the final years of the nineteenth century, the government decided that army regiments should be linked by name to the area from which they predominantly came. This, they thought, would help recruitment, men being more likely to volunteer for a regiment which bore the name of the county in which they lived than, for example, the 68th Foot although the regiment had, by this time, become known as the 68th (Durham) Foot. In 1881, the 68th (Durham) Foot was amalgamated with the 106th Foot to form the Durham Light Infantry (DLI). There were, at first, two battalions, each of between eight hundred and one thousand men from all ranks. The idea was that one of these would serve abroad, usually somewhere in the British Empire, and the other would remain at home. The DLI's first regimental headquarters were in Newcastle-upon-Tyne, shared with the Royal Northumberland Fusiliers, but in 1884 they moved to Sunderland.

From the time of its foundation to the early years of the twentieth century, soldiers of the Durham Light Infantry found themselves in many parts of the world. Sometimes they were sent to trouble spots to deal with threats to the British Empire and at other times they carried out garrison duties at imperial outposts, ready to react to local threats if problems surfaced. It's hard for us today, when Great Britain plays a relatively minor role on the global stage, to envisage a world in which a very small island kingdom ruled over one-fifth of the planet's population, living in almost a quarter of the earth's total land surface. Whether or not this was a good thing is a matter of constant debate.

This then was the world into which the Durham Light Infantry were born. In 1885 they performed garrison duty in Gibraltar before being sent to Egypt where they fought alongside Egyptian troops to defeat the Sudanese Dervishes at the battle of Ginnis. The DLI have always been closely associated with India and performed garrison duties there for many years. India was the British Empire's "jewel in the crown" and one of the most trouble-strewn of her possessions with local populations desperate to throw off British rule. Nevertheless, there was usually time for sport and leisure and the DLI dominated the Army Polo Cup during the closing years of the twentieth century.

It wasn't long, however, before they found themselves involved in another major conflict. By 1899 there were four DLI battalions and all four fought in the Boer War in South Africa between 1899 and 1901. There had been a shorter conflict almost twenty years earlier but this was a prolonged war involving thousands of troops from either side.

South Africa was an important colony for the British because it was rich in minerals, especially gold and diamonds, and the Cape of Good Hope controlled one of the most important shipping and trade routes between Europe and the East. South Africa's first European settlers were Dutch, and the Dutch East India Company, an important and successful trading organisation, established an outpost in what is now Cape Town at the end of the seventeenth century. One hundred years later the British arrived and took control of the Cape Colony. By this time, the Dutch settlements had spread hundreds of miles inland and, in the final years of the nineteenth century, began to establish their own independent republics. The British didn't want to see this happen and the Boer War was fought so that Britain could regain control of the whole of South Africa from the Boers, many of whom were farmers who spoke their own language, Afrikaans, which is similar to Dutch.

This was, therefore, a war between two groups of settlers but it did not involve the native Africans, who outnumbered the European settlers but had few rights and little or no power until the end of the Twentieth Century. It was a very tough war, with many casualties on either side. Eventually, however, the British Empire came out victorious, with the DLI playing an important role. The most unsavoury aspect of the conflict was the deaths of more than twenty thousand Boers in one of the earliest examples of concentration camps. We shall look at their twentieth-century German equivalent in Chapter Three.

The start of the new century saw the world becoming an increasingly unstable place. The aggressive growth of the German Empire, and the decline of the Habsburg (Austria-Hungary) and Ottoman Empires, were viewed with suspicion and alarm by Europe's other great powers, Great Britain, France and Russia. Great Britain eyed the Ottoman Empire as a possible area of expansion and Germany could see possibilities of increasing her empire through further territorial gains in Central and Eastern Europe. The French had been defeated by the Prussians (now the

Figure 3: The Boer War Memorial at Durham Cathedral.

Germans) in 1870–71 and lost territory to them. The sides were jockeying for position. The countries responded to this unrest by increasing the size of their armies. In Great Britain this was done by recruiting soldiers to join the Territorial Army (TA). These were part-time soldiers who trained for combat at weekends and who were held in reserve until they were needed. In the early years of the twentieth century, a number of these TA units were raised in North East England.

The opening years of the century were relatively quiet. DLI troops carried out garrison duties at Cork in the south of Ireland (then part of the United Kingdom). However, this was very much the calm before the storm because, in August 1914, war broke out. The immediate cause was the assassination of the heir to the imperial Austria-Hungary throne Archduke Franz Ferdinand in Sarajevo (in present-day Bosnia). This happened several weeks before war broke out but provided the match to light the fire. The actual causes were far more complicated. They involved a mixture of treaties, misunderstandings, mobilisation of armies and the settling of old scores. Anyone interested in this should read *The Sleepwalkers* by Christopher Clark or, for an alternative point of view, *Catastrophe: Europe Goes to War* by Max Hastings. There were plenty of people in Britain who did not want to go to war, but what finally persuaded the politicians to declare war on Germany and her allies was the German invasion of Belgium in late summer 1914. Britain had signed a treaty guaranteeing Belgium neutrality as long ago as 1839 and was now expected to back up that guarantee with action, as well as supporting her allies France and Russia.

The First World War (or the Great War as it was known at first) was fought between the Allies (the British Empire, France, Russia and, later, the United States) and the Central Powers (Germany, Austria-Hungary and the Ottoman Empire). Other countries fought on both sides. There were campaigns all over the world, at sea and, for the first time, there was war in the air. The war is best remembered for the terrible slaughter on the Western Front in parts of Belgium and Northern France and it was to this part of Europe that soldiers of the Durham Light Infantry sailed on 7 September 1914. They were almost immediately in action, fighting a fierce rearguard action against the Germans at the first Battle of Aisne in France. The Durhams, as they were now known, quickly established themselves as a crack regiment, a reputation they sustained for more than fifty years. As casualties mounted on the Western Front, more and more soldiers crossed to France including the DLI Territorials and, from 1916, many were forced to join up after parliament passed an act making conscription compulsory. By the end of the war, many teenagers were fighting for their lives in Northern France and elsewhere.

The first Durham-born soldier to receive the Victoria Cross was Private Thomas Kenny who was honoured after showing conspicuous gallantry at Armentieres in Northern France in November 1915. Kenny was born in South Wingate near Peterlee and served with the 13th Battalion DLI. After the war he returned to his former job as a miner. He died in Durham in 1948 at the age of sixty-six.

One of the most remarkable and tragic stories to emerge from the First World War was that of the Bradford family. Amy Bradford lost three of her sons in the First World War. George, one of those honoured, was in the Royal Navy and was awarded the Victoria Cross but the youngest of the three, Roland, was a junior officer in the Durham Light Infantry. He received the Military Cross for gallantry in February 1915 and the VC when he was temporarily in command of the 6th Battalion DLI at Le Sars in October 1916.

Just over a year later he was killed at the Battle of Cambrai. He was just twenty-five years of age.

In Belgium and France the campaigns became battles of attrition with both sides facing each other across no-man's land over hundreds of miles of trenches. Here the Durham soldiers, many of them small in stature and used to burrowing underground in the coal mines, were particularly effective. They fought like tigers alongside comrades from many other regiments at places whose very names conjure up pictures of mud and death:

- Ypres (where poison gas was used for the first time in the war)
- The Somme
- Loos
- Arras (where on 9 April 1917, the Durhams and other Allied troops drove the Germans back four thousand yards)
- Messines
- Cambrai (history's first great tank battle)
- Passchendaele

Other Durham soldiers saw action on the Balkan front (at Thessalonica fighting the Turks), Italy, Russia and the north-west frontier of India. When the guns finally fell silent on 11 November 1918, sixteen million had lost their lives and a further twenty million were wounded, many of them incapacitated for life. Thirteen thousand Durham soldiers died in the war. Thousands more were wounded, many of them seriously. There was hardly a community in the whole of the county which was untouched by the loss of loved ones. An indication of the enormous contribution of the Durhams to the eventual victory for the Allies was that six Victoria Crosses were awarded to members of the DLI.

There were then twenty years of peace before the Second World War broke out in September 1939. In Britain, as elsewhere in Europe, these two decades were, for many, times of poverty and misery. North East England suffered particularly badly. The main industries, coal mining, steel making and ship building, declined disastrously and many thousands of jobs were lost. In the old industrial areas, the situation remained unchanged until the outbreak of war. Recovery began in South East England but, in many other areas, hunger and despair remained. Roy Hattersley in his book *Borrowed Time: The Story of Britain between the Wars* describes this era particularly well as does Juliet Gardiner in her brilliant book *The Thirties*. The images of these twenty years, men loitering pointlessly outside labour exchanges, hunger marches and thin faced men, women and children staring hopelessly into camera lenses, remain as a poignant reminder of those terrible times.

Under these circumstances, it's hardly surprising that the Durham Light Infantry had little difficulty in recruiting soldiers. Central and Western Europe had had enough of war and there were no major conflicts. But, for Britain, there was an Empire to protect and peace-keeping duties to perform. Immediately after the Great War, the DLI were briefly part of the army of occupation in parts of Germany before moving to Northern Ireland in 1925. The south of Ireland had become partly independent from the United Kingdom in 1920 but the threat of unrest remained and British troops carrying out garrison duties in Northern Ireland remained a necessity. Other DLI troops found themselves in India, Egypt and even in China, which had been invaded by the Japanese in 1931 and remained at war with her eastern neighbours until 1945.

The need for a strong, well-trained army in Britain became increasingly important. The chaos in Germany after the Great War led to what seemed to be endless times of poverty and unemployment. There were years of unrest in villages, towns and cities as extreme political parties, taking full advantage of the unstable political situation, fought each other for the right to put Germany back on track. On the left were the communists and on the right the Nazis, whose leader, Adolf Hitler, became Chancellor of Germany in January 1933. He took just over three years to sort out what he saw as problems at home, including the suppression of all of his political opponents, especially the communists, as well as embarking on a campaign to persecute the Jews, before turning his attention to foreign policy. At the end of the Great War, treaties had been signed at Versailles near Paris which had, amongst other things, deprived Germany of some of the territory she had held in 1914. For example, the German city of Danzig (today Gdansk) had been taken away from her and given to the Poles in order for that country to have access to the Baltic Sea. Danzig did not actually become part of Poland but was designated a neutral city by the peacemakers, to be governed by the League of Nations, forerunner of today's United Nations. The area south of Danzig, which became known as the Polish Corridor, and parts of Upper Silesia were also given to the Poles. Austria, which had split from Hungary at the end of the war, was anxious to join Germany but the peacemakers were totally against this and the union of the two was prohibited. The politicians who redrew the map of Europe after the war managed to place several thousand German speaking people inside the new state of Czechoslovakia. All of these grievances gave Hitler the excuse to start remonstrating about the injustices of the Treaty of Versailles. In 1938 he seized Austria and then began to demand that those parts of Czechoslovakia where Germans were living be incorporated within Germany. Britain and France, the two leading European powers, were desperate to avoid being plunged into another war and, at Munich in September 1938, gave Hitler what he wanted. When Hitler occupied the rest of Czechoslovakia in March 1939, he soon made it clear that his next target was Danzig, and Britain and France told Poland that they would come to her aid if she was attacked. So when German troops crossed the Polish border in September 1939, Britain and France declared war. This is a very simplified account of events. *The Origins of the Second World War* by A. J. P. Taylor is an excellent book and my own novel *The Blue Pencil* gives an account of the political games played by the British government in an attempt to avoid war.

The very significant part played by the DLI in the war is covered in the next chapter. It's enough to say at this stage that they fought with great courage and success in many of the leading theatres of war: in France (1940), North Africa (1941), Italy (1942–5), Burma (1943–5) and from D-Day to the final surrender of Germany (1944–5).

After the war, the Durhams were part of the forces of occupation in Germany and helped with the rebuilding of Europe. More than thirty million of the fifty-five million deaths worldwide had occurred in Europe and had left the continent in a dreadful state. Civil unrest, famine and disease were rife. After the Great War allied troops had only briefly occupied Germany but from 1945 onwards there was a heavy presence of British, French, American and Russian troops providing an army of occupation, each country being given its own zone of responsibility. In 1949, the German state split into two. The Russian zone became the German Democratic Republic (GDR), a communist state, and the remaining zones became the Federal Republic of Germany (FRG). Berlin was in the Russian sector but an agreement at the post-war peace conference divided the city into four separate sectors, these again being under the control of the United States, Great Britain, France and the Soviet Union. Relationships between the Allies quickly deteriorated after the end of the war and a "Cold" War dominated international politics until the collapse of communism in Eastern Europe in 1989. The main players in this war of words and threats were the USA on one side and the USSR (present-day Russia and the former Soviet republics) on the other. Berlin was the Cold War's most dangerous place and DLI troops were stationed there before, during and after 1961 when the Berlin Wall, which divided Communist Berlin (the east) from the remainder of the city (the west), was built.

The Durhams fought in the Korean War as part of a United Nations force trying to repel the invasion of South Korea by the communist North (1950–3). The North Koreans were heavily supported by the Chinese and, to a lesser extent, the Russians. The result of the war was indecisive and the Durhams spent the rest of the 1950s dealing with trouble spots within the British Empire where the natives of many of our colonies were fighting to overthrow British rule. They found themselves in Aden (1957), Cyprus (1958) and, on and off throughout the first half of the decade, in Egypt where the pro-Russian president Gamal Nasser was threatening to seize control of the internationally owned Suez Canal.

The final campaign in the illustrious history of the DLI came in Borneo in 1965. Malaysia (formerly Malaya) was a British colony until achieving independence in 1957. The war was a dispute between Malaysia and the neighbouring state of Indonesia about who controlled the northern part of Borneo. The Durhams were one of several British regiments who fought against the Indonesians in the jungles of Borneo. The war ended in 1966 with both sides recognising the disputed territory being Malaysian.

Just a year later the government conducted a review of the British Army. They decided that there was no longer a need for a large number of regiments. Most of the colonies of the British Empire had become independent and, despite the ongoing threat of the Cold War, it seemed unlikely that a major conflict would break

Figure 4: A Bugler of the Durham Light Infantry during the Korean War, depicted in bronze in Durham Market Place. (© Trustees of The Regimental and Chattels Charity of the former Durham Light Infantry.)

out. After the review, four light infantry regiments, Somerset and Cornwall, Yorkshire, Shropshire, and Durham were amalgamated to form a new regiment, the Light Infantry. In February 2007, the Light Infantry merged with a number of others to form the Rifles and it is in that regiment that the DLI live on.

On 12 December 1968, Princess Alexandra, Colonel-in-Chief of the Durham Light Infantry attended the final parade of the regiment on Durham's Palace Green. The regimental colours were laid up in Durham Cathedral. Today the regiment is remembered in the cathedral through the Durham Light Infantry Chapel which houses, amongst other important items, is the Book of Remembrance. Outside the cathedral is the DLI Memorial Garden. Near Durham Railway Station is the outstanding Durham Light Infantry Museum where the illustrious history of this famous regiment is superbly told.

Many famous people have worn the uniform of the DLI. Those gallant men who won the Victoria Cross are listed at the end of this book. Other notable people include the following:

- **General Sir Peter de la Billière** was Commander-in-Chief of the British forces in the first Gulf War (1990).
- **Lieutenant Leslie Phillips MBE**, who seems to have appeared in just about every British comedy film in the nineteen fifties and sixties, served briefly in the Second World War.
- **Private Malcolm Sargent**, later Sir Malcolm, conducted the Promenade Concerts in London's Royal Albert Hall for almost twenty years until his death in 1967. He served in the First World War and was a graduate of Durham University.
- **Private Bill Nicholson OBE** was an English international footballer who in later life managed Tottenham Hotspur, when they became the first football club in the twentieth century to win the FA Cup and Football League Division One "double".

Figure 5: The regimental colours hanging in
the DLI Chapel in Durham Cathedral.

Figure 6: The DLI Chapel in Durham Cathedral.

This is a brief history of the DLI. For further reading I suggest *The Durham Light Infantry* by William Moore or, for a more detailed history, *Faithful: The Story of the Light Infantry* by S. G. P. Ward and Nigel Poett.

When Field Marshall Montgomery, who had led the British forces (including the Durhams) to victory over the Germans at the battle of El Alamein in Egypt (1942), heard that the DLI was to be amalgamated with other regiments he said:

> I cannot mention them all, but I feel very sad about one, the Durham Light Infantry, the regiment which marched with me from Alamein to Germany and never put a foot wrong.

A fitting tribute from a great soldier to a great regiment.

CHAPTER TWO

BATTLEFIELDS
The Second World War 1939–1945

It is a magnificent regiment, steady as a rock in
battle and absolutely reliable on all other occasions.
Field Marshall Bernard Montgomery

The Second World War began on 1 September 1939 when Germany invaded Poland. The British and the French had previously promised Poland that they would come to her aid if she was attacked. As a result, Britain and France declared war on Germany on 3 September 1939. The five-year-long war was fought on four continents: Europe, Africa, Asia and America, on the Atlantic, Pacific, Indian and Arctic oceans and in the air everywhere. When it was over in August 1945, the number of dead was roughly equivalent to the present population of England. The major areas in which the conflict took place were:

- **Western Europe:** At first it was just the British and Commonwealth troops who fought against the Germans but, after Germany had overrun large parts of Europe, some citizens of those countries who had escaped fought on the Allied side. (The main Allies were Britain and France. Later

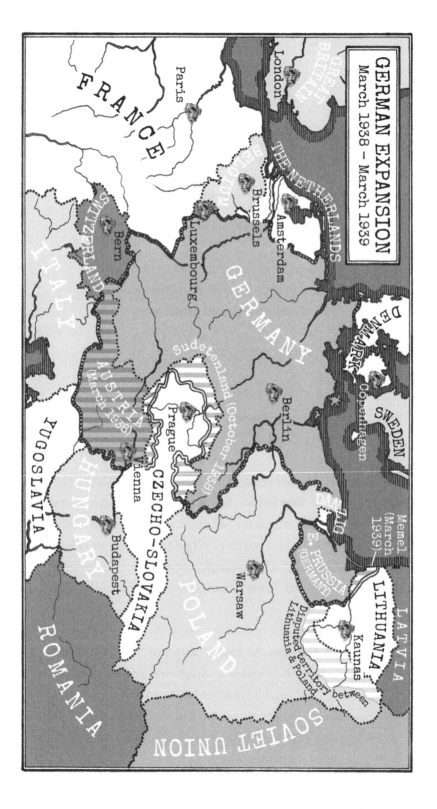

in the war the United States and the Soviet Union fought on the Allied side as well as people from smaller countries.) The enemy were the Germans and the Italians.

- **Eastern Europe:** The Soviet Union (present-day Russia plus other former Soviet states like the Ukraine) against the Germans who included in their forces citizens of those countries which they had conquered or were threatening (e.g. Romania).
- **The Pacific:** The USA against the Empire of Japan.
- **South East Asia:** British and Commonwealth troops, China and the USA fighting against the Empire of Japan.
- **North Africa and the Middle East:** British and Commonwealth troops and the USA fighting against the Germans and Italians.
- **The Atlantic and Arctic Oceans:** British, Commonwealth, Soviet and USA naval and merchant ships battling against German U-boats and battleships.
- **America:** Only in as much as the USA's war with Japan started when the Japanese attacked Pearl Harbour in December 1941.

In most, but not all, of these theatres of war, soldiers from the DLI fought with great courage and determination, undoubtedly helping to win the war for the Allies. The DLI was a collection of battalions, each of which was up to one thousand strong. Different battalions fought in different parts of the world. Even within one particular battalion, subdivisions (companies) might be sent to fight in different areas of the same campaign. The number of battalions increased as the war went on. Some were professional soldiers, others were volunteers, whilst some will have been conscripted. Occasionally, battalions were combined to form a new fighting force. From time to time, battalions were disbanded and the soldiers incorporated within other battalions.

The number of troops in action around the world would depend on the situation in that theatre of war at any one time. Almost always, the Durhams fought not alone but as part of a larger unit, a Brigade or an Army where they were alongside soldiers of other regiments. Nobody was ever thrust into war without proper training. Some of the Durhams never even reached the battlefields. Some were being held in reserve or kept in England to carry out important defensive duties. For the purpose of the story that follows, the Durhams or the DLI will be used to describe the role played by soldiers of that regiment all over the world. A far more detailed history of the part played by the Durham Light Infantry in the Second World War can be found in *The DLI at War: The History of the Durham Light Infantry 1939–1945*. This excellent book was written by David Rissik, an officer of the DLI who served during the Second World War.

France and Belgium: September 1939 to June 1945

After Britain and France had declared war on Germany, the Allies assumed that Northern France and Belgium would be the main theatre of war, as it had been between 1914 and 1918. The French, anticipating this, had built a series of forts, linked by tunnels, along the length of their frontier with Germany. It was called the Maginot Line and was constructed between 1930 and 1940. Unfortunately the Maginot Line stopped at the Belgian frontier and it was here in Northern France that the Durhams found themselves in September

1939. That winter was bitterly cold and the soldiers "dug in" near Lille, expecting a German invasion at any time. This period was known as the Phoney War. It came to an abrupt end in April 1940, when the Germans invaded and occupied Norway and Denmark. Germany defeated those two countries and it was now expected that France would be next.

So it proved. A month after the attacks on Norway and Denmark, the German armed forces (the Wehrmacht) swept into the Netherlands, Belgium and France. They didn't attack the Maginot Line, but sent forces to confront the Allies in Belgium. The British and French forces were strong, but had left a gap in their defences where only a small force faced the densely forested area of Belgium known as the Ardennes. Nobody on the Allied side believed that the Wehrmacht would attack here. The woods were so dense and the roads so narrow it seemed impossible for tanks to get through. But they did and soon the Allied soldiers found themselves threatened with being surrounded by the several German armies.

The Durhams first saw action in the middle of May near the River Dyle in Belgium. The Allies had advanced into Belgium to face what they thought was the strongest of the German armies, but the main German thrust had come through the Ardennes and they had fallen into the trap laid for them by the German generals.

The Durhams fought hard and courageously at the Dyle and resisted fiercely. They were up against German tanks and armour with fast moving motorised infantry supported by air attacks. It was the DLI's first taste of *Blitzkrieg* which the Germans had used so successfully in overwhelming Poland the previous autumn. Eventually the DLI were forced to withdraw, but not before Captain Dickie Annand from South Shields had earned one of the Second World War's first Victoria Crosses.

By this time it was clear that the battle for France was lost and orders were given to head for the sea and be taken home by ship. It was uncertain how many would escape but what was certain was that heavy gear would have to be left behind. To make sure that the Germans wouldn't be able to make use of what was left, the Allied troops destroyed hundreds of tanks, various other forms of motorised transport and field guns.

It seemed possible that by 20 May the Germans would break through the Dunkirk perimeter, which was protecting the retreating British and French troops, and that nobody would escape. Their triumphant march to victory was halted at Arras in North West France by British forces which included two battalions of the DLI, the 74th Tank Regiment, the Northumberland Fusiliers and the 12th Lancers. There was virtually no chance of victory. The Germans had massive air support. The Allies had very little with most of the RAF returned to England to protect their homeland against the German invasion, which many thought was now inevitable. However, such was the ferocity of the Allied attack, the Wehrmacht were taken aback. Despite the eventual and necessary withdrawal, the Battle of Arras did achieve something important; it slowed the Germans down. For the first time since the war had begun, their hitherto unstoppable march through Poland, Belgium, Holland, Luxembourg and France had been halted. They wondered what lay ahead for them. What was the strength of the enemy? The Germans considered briefly that they themselves might be outflanked and ultimately surrounded, so they paused and checked with their intelligence people about the strength of the opposition. The answer wasn't long in coming. The Germans had long since cracked the feeble French signal codes so the Wehrmacht quickly knew that their enemies were heading for the sea. The advance was resumed but, during the twenty-hour lull in the fighting, tens of thousands of Allied troops had been able to make their way to Dunkirk.

As June approached, the situation on the Allied side was total chaos. Many soldiers were lost, having been separated from their battalions during the fighting. Two Durham soldiers even dressed as French civilians and walked through the German lines to safety. Retreating columns of troops were frequently attacked by the Luftwaffe. The whole of Northern France seemed to be on the move. Apart from the disciplined Wehrmacht and the shambolic Allies, thousands of French non-combatants were trying to head for safety, clogging the roads with lorries, vans, cars, bicycles, prams and pushcarts.

The evacuation from the beaches began on 27 May and lasted for just over a week. The majority of the Durhams arrived on 1 June. For all the troops there was a period of nervous waiting on the beaches with the Luftwaffe appearing from time to time and spraying the troops with machine-gun fire. Less than eight thousand men were evacuated on the first day and it quickly became obvious that the Royal Navy didn't have enough ships to ferry all of the soldiers to safety. Operation Dynamo, to take as many off the beaches as possible, now swung into action and hundreds of small craft: fishing boats, pleasure boats, dredgers, tug boats, paddle steamers, river craft and life boats amongst them, headed across the Channel to rescue the soldiers. Some of these "little ships" never returned but many more did so that, by the time that the evacuation ended on 4 June 1940, more than three hundred and thirty thousand British and French troops had been rescued. Leaving aside the bravery of the soldiers in Northern France and Belgium and the crews of the rescuing boats and ships, the French campaign of 1940 was a total disaster for the Allies. Winston Churchill, the British Prime Minister, while praising the troops and their rescuers, reminded everyone that no war was ever won in retreat. Within a week, France had surrendered and Britain stood alone against the might of Nazi Germany.

Amongst the last to leave Dunkirk's beaches were soldiers from the DLI. They would be amongst the first Regiments to set foot on the beaches of France on D-Day, 6 June 1944.

The planned invasion of Britain by Germany in the summer and autumn of 1940 (Operation Sea Lion) was postponed by Hitler after the Luftwaffe failed to gain control of the skies over England. They came off second best to the Hurricanes and Spitfires of the Royal Air Force in the Battle of Britain. From September 1940 to May 1941, British cities were bombed by the Luftwaffe. Thousands of lives were lost and tens of thousands of houses, factories and warehouses were levelled. Docks were destroyed and put out of action. In the Atlantic Ocean tons of merchant shipping bringing vital supplies to Britain were sunk by German submarines (U-boats). Further military disasters followed as British and Commonwealth troops were thrown out of Crete and Greece by the Germans. Already, however, another theatre of war had opened up. It was a period of the war when the DLI were to play a major triumphant role.

The Desert War 1940–1943

"The Desert was made for war." So said Laurence Olivier as he introduced an episode of *The World at War* (1973), a twenty-six part television series. Indeed, the desert *was* made for war. There wasn't much there: a few isolated settlements, some railway lines and very makeshift roads. The rest was just sand. There were no large towns to reduce to rubble and no innocent civilians to kill. Just sand.

The three colonial powers in North Africa in 1940 were the French in the west, the Italians in Libya and Abyssinia, and the British in Egypt. In June 1940, Italy declared war on the British Empire. Mussolini, the Italian dictator, had been an ally of Hitler and Germany for some time, but waited to see how the Battle for France was going before actually entering the war. He was now certain that Germany would win the war and he wanted to sit alongside the Führer at the post-war conference table so that any rich pickings, like more North African territory, might fall his way.

Mussolini's first goal was to drive the British out of Egypt. This would give him control of the Suez Canal, a vital link for Great Britain with her possessions in the Far East and Australia. Italy's second target was the oil fields of the Middle East. Seizure of these would not only give Germany and Italy much-needed fuel, but would deny Britain essential petrol to drive her tanks, ships, aeroplanes and other forms of mechanised transport.

The 1st battalion of the DLI had been in China at the outbreak of war but, even before Italy joined Hitler, the Allied generals and politicians recognised that Egypt must be defended at all costs. So the Durhams set off for Suez where they arrived on 30 January 1940. Italy's entry into the war six months later meant that the British troops, including the DLI, had to march westwards to face the Italians along the Egypt–Libya border.

The Italians made the first move. They had three hundred thousand troops ready to conquer Egypt. Against them were just thirty-six thousand British and Commonwealth troops. The Italians crossed the border and marched expectantly into Egypt. Mussolini, seeing himself as a modern-day Roman Emperor, began to plan a triumphant victory parade through Cairo.

The Italians had already suffered some misfortune. While they were waiting to invade Egypt, small British raiding parties seized a number of the enemy inside Libya. This included a senior Italian General who was captured, together with his mistress, in a car. The Italian Army's Commander-in-Chief was shot down in an aeroplane by his own men, presumably by mistake! Despite this they marched into Egypt and paused at Sidi Baranni where they built defensive positions comprising forts and trenches.

They remained there for a time while attention switched to Greece, which they invaded in October 1940. This meant fewer supplies for their North African armies. In Greece, the Italians were quickly in retreat and were pursued by the Greeks into Albania, which the Italians had overrun in April 1940. Back in Egypt, the Allies, including the Durhams, prepared to attack the Italians (Operation Compass). On 9 December 1940, the Allies attacked the Italian position at Sidi Baranni and soon had the enemy in retreat. For the loss of six hundred and twenty-four casualties, they captured thirty-eight thousand Italians. The British and Commonwealth troops then crossed the border into Libya and captured a further forty-five thousand enemy soldiers on 6 January 1941. The Allies then took Tobruk, a strategically important Libyan port, which would help supply the British troops from ships in the Mediterranean and Malta. Another twenty-five thousand Italians found themselves behind barbed wire.

In mid-January 1941, the Italians were driven out of Abyssinia and by mid-February they were beaten. They had fought poorly. Over one hundred thousand of their troops were prisoners of war. Despite having fought courageously during the First World War, the Italians provided much less stern opposition over thirty years later. Mussolini usually chose soft targets like Abyssinia and Albania for his aggression. Hitler, however, recognised the strategic importance of the desert and in February 1941, sent General Erwin Rommel, one of the heroes of the conquest of France, to Libya, with an advance guard of soldiers who were to become known as the Afrika Corps. The next phase of the desert war would be much tougher.

Rommel's arrival in Libya showed just how much Hitler valued the desert. Not only would victory give him access to the Middle East's oil, all-out war would tie up British troops. Hitler had hoped that his ally, Italy, might do this job but wasn't at all surprised when they capitulated and Rommel was sent to bail out what was left of the Italian army. The German general took a little while to take stock of the situation. On 31 March 1941, he attacked and immediately drove the British and Commonwealth forces back across the border into Egypt. Then, collecting the remnants of the Italian army, he turned his attention to Tobruk. Like the Allies, he recognised the importance of the Libyan port and Germany was especially dependent on having a port in the Eastern Mediterranean because they would otherwise have had to bring their supplies across the desert for almost a thousand miles. The Allied forces defending Tobruk were mostly Australian. Rommel's ground forces bombed and shelled the Libyan port for two hundred and forty days, reducing it to rubble. The Allies' Eighth Army, which included several thousand troops from the DLI, fought their way through the enemy troops to lift the siege in November 1941.

Rommel then put together a plan to drive the Allies out of North Africa. It was extremely ambitious because Hitler had withdrawn some troops and equipment in order to send them to the Eastern Front where Germany were involved in a war with the Soviet Union. The Germans and Italians still had problems with their supplies and so their first target, in June of 1942, was to attack Tobruk. The ferocity of the German attack, combined with the bombing support from what aircraft could be spared, gave Rommel a swift victory.

Four thousand tons of oil fell into German hands. For the Allies it was a total disaster.

The Germans pushed the Allied troops back into Egypt who paused at the railway junction of El Alamein. During the retreat, Private Adam Wakenshaw, a Newcastle-upon-Tyne born member of the DLI, was killed after fighting courageously despite being seriously injured. He became the second Durham man in the Second World War to be awarded the Victoria Cross.

In Cairo, diplomats began burning documents, expecting the enemy at any time. Mussolini arrived in Libya with a grey horse, which he proposed to ride in the victory parade in Cairo. Throughout the summer, there were many skirmishes between the two armies but the only significant victory came when Australian troops beat off some of their Italian counterparts who faced them at El Alamein. The war was stagnant and, despite his successes to date, Rommel showed no signs of being able to break the stubborn Allied defence. Winston Churchill, the British Prime Minister, was anxious for action. He visited the desert armies in Egypt in August and was immediately critical of the defensive attitude of the Generals. He sacked a couple and put General Bernard Montgomery in charge of the Eighth Army. It was a crucial decision for both the Allies and the DLI. For the Allies, Montgomery was an inspired choice who changed the course of the war and for the Durhams a general who led many of them from the desert of North Africa to the surrender of enemy forces in Northern Germany.

The stage was set for the biggest battle of the war to date. Montgomery spent September building up his strength: more men, more tanks and new weapons. Facing him was Rommel who, despite his earlier successes, was still struggling with supplies. The Navy ruled the Mediterranean and the RAF was in charge in the skies. The Germans couldn't make a move without the Allied High

Command knowing about it. Code-breakers at Bletchley Park (near present-day Milton Keynes) were intercepting and decoding the German radio signals.

The Battle of El Alamein started on 23 October 1942 with a massive barrage of guns aimed at the German lines. The Germans resisted and a second major offensive was ordered for 2 November. Three DLI battalions joined the Eighth Army who, after a three-hour bombardment of the German lines, advanced towards the enemy and soon had them running for their lives. To make matters worse for the Germans, the Americans had now entered the war and a combined US–Great Britain force had landed in North Africa while the Battle of El Alamein was raging. Rommel, now retreating to the west, was trapped between the advancing Eighth Army and the Allied force advancing eastwards. Durham soldiers were part of both sides of the pincer, with three battalions in the Eighth Army and the 16th Battalion landing in Tunisia in January to fight alongside the Americans.

The Germans were, however, no pushovers and they fought so ferociously in retreat that it wasn't until 13 May 1943 that the Germans and Italians were finally defeated and removed from North Africa. One of the toughest fights came at Mareth, in Tunisia, where the DLI came up against some of the strongest Italian resistance of the campaign. Eventually the enemy forces were broken and the troops rested before the next phase of the war began.

Sicily and Italy 1943–45

The war had been tough for the Allies, especially the citizens who had endured countless air raids on their cities and towns between September 1940 and May 1941. Thousands of innocent lives had been lost and countless buildings destroyed. However, by the time the Durhams embarked on their next test in July 1943, the picture had changed. The DLI had distinguished itself in the retreat from France in May and June 1940 and acquitted themselves superbly in the desert war, especially the great battle of El Alamein. Though nobody knew it at the time, the tide of the war had turned decisively against the Germans. In the two years up to the middle of 1943, a number of events had taken place which together would result in the defeat of Germany in 1945.

- Germany had invaded the Soviet Union in 1941. Russia became Britain's ally in the fight against Hitler.
- Japan had attacked the USA in December 1941. Shortly after this, Germany declared war on the USA, adding the Americans, with all their manpower and resources, to the Anglo-Soviet alliance.
- The Germans suffered their first major defeat at El Alamein and soon found themselves driven out of Africa altogether.
- The German Sixth Army had been crushed at Stalingrad, allowing the Russians to go on the offensive and begin driving the Germans back to their own borders.

However, although the course of the war in parts of Europe and North Africa was beginning to point to an eventual Allied victory, almost two years of exceptionally hard fighting remained. Millions more soldiers, sailors, airmen, men, women and children would die.

Countless cities and towns would be reduced to rubble. Buildings that had stood for a thousand years or more would be totally destroyed. The Durhams' next campaign would show just how tough the road would be.

Sicily was the next stop for the DLI. The 6th and 9th battalions would be the assault brigade whose job it was to secure the beachhead to enable more troops, heavy equipment and other supplies to be brought ashore unhindered. The landings which took place at dawn on 10 July 1943 were preceded by an aerial bombardment. Paratroopers were landed in the Sicilian countryside. The invasion fleet had set sail from Malta, Tunisia and other North African ports. The Allied invasion force consisted primarily of British and Commonwealth forces and Americans. A storm had hindered the voyage and many soldiers were sick in the landing craft that had deposited them on the beach.

The Durhams' target was Avola in the south-east corner of Sicily. At first, many soldiers found themselves in the wrong place but quick reorganisation meant that they were able to take the town of Avola and hoist the regimental flag above the railway station. There was little opposition from the Italians and the local people, as soon as they recognised that the newcomers were the Allies and not more Germans, welcomed them with open arms.

As in North Africa, the Germans were much tougher fighters than the Italians and there were some terrific battles in the Sicilian olive groves and densely planted vineyards. One of the Durhams' most difficult assignments had been to relieve a platoon of paratroopers who had seized a strategically important bridge over the River Simeto at Plimsole. The Germans had reacted quickly and sent a force to retake the bridge. The paras were just about hanging on when the Durhams arrived after a thirty-five mile march in heavy kit and high summer temperatures. The troops immediately came under sustained fire and they engaged the Wehrmacht in deadly hand-to-hand fighting. Both sides lost many men but the DLI emerged victorious. They secured the bridge and then marched to the city of Catania where another rapturous reception from the local people awaited them.

The Americans had also fought bravely and successfully meaning that, by the middle of August, Sicily had been completely cleared of Germans, although many Wehrmacht troops had escaped across the straits of Messina to the Italian mainland. The three DLI battalions, which had played such a heroic role in the conquest of Sicily now prepared themselves to be part of the force to invade Italy. To their delight and surprise, they were shipped home to prepare for an even greater challenge that lay ahead.

While the three DLI battalions were sailing home, the 16th Battalion was taking part in the invasion of Italy. The troops embarked from Bizerta in Tunisia on 8 September 1943 and landed at Salerno, south of Naples. Three years had passed since British troops had been on the European mainland but the battles were hard just as they had been in Northern France and Belgium in the summer of 1940. The Germans put up a tremendous fight at Salerno and it took more than a week to secure the beachhead. Eventually the Wehrmacht withdrew northwards. The Allies' next target was the port of Naples. By the time they set off in this direction, Italy was out of the war. Their dictator Mussolini had been arrested and stripped of office and the new government sued for peace. In Naples, anticipating the Allies' arrival, the population rose up and, with the help of the local resistance, kicked the Germans out. On 1 October the Allied armies entered Naples in triumph.

It all seemed rather easy. The Italians had not put up much resistance and now they were out of the war. The Germans had fought hard but now they too were retreating northwards. It seemed possible that Allied troops would be entering Rome before the end of the year. Winston Churchill had described Italy as the "soft underbelly of Europe" and in October 1943 it seemed he was right. Hitler, however, was having none of it and he poured troops into Italy, seized Rome and then ordered the setting up of a strong defensive line to the south. The Führer's generals had advised against this, warning him that this would weaken Germany's forces facing Russia and also leaving their armies in France under strength to face the cross-channel invasion which they felt certain would happen in 1944. Hitler argued that keeping Allied troops pinned down in Italy would weaken them elsewhere.

The result was that the Germans mounted an incredibly fearsome resistance in a line across Italy to the south of Rome. To make matters worse, the winter of 1943–4 was very wet and fields and roads turned into quagmires. The Germans held all the strategic positions in the mountains of central Italy, and what they called their *winter line* ran across the country about eighty miles to the south of Rome. The best-known battle of this campaign was the five-month-long siege of Monte Cassino, a mountainside town above which stood a Benedictine abbey where the Germans had positioned themselves and poured withering fire on the Allied armies below. Despite several very large bombing raids, the abbey didn't fall to the Allies until May 1944. What was left of the German defenders withdrew and the road to Rome was open.

The Durhams meanwhile had been facing equally strong German resistance further to the east. The Wehrmacht were tough to beat but the British Eighth Army did make some headway before the DLI Battalion was relieved in February. They enjoyed several months of rest and training in Cairo before many returned to Italy in July. By this time Rome had fallen to the Allies and, shortly after the Durhams' arrival, Florence fell. They spent the autumn of 1944 fighting the Germans who had established a new defensive line in Northern Italy. DLI troops played only a limited part in this campaign but did succeed in driving the Germans out of the strategically important town of Cesena, north of Florence. Some Germans were too slow to react to the evacuation of the town and seven of them were captured by Durham soldiers while enjoying a shave in a barber's shop.

Shortly after this, the DLI were reassigned to Greece where civil war was brewing and the soldiers' job was to keep the peace. This they did successfully but a full-scale civil war erupted just after the end of the Second World War. Then it was back to Italy for the final three weeks of the war. The Germans were, by now, in full retreat and finally laid down their arms when the war in Europe ended on 8 May 1945. For the 16th Battalion of the DLI it was post-war occupation duties for a short while in Vienna before the battalion was disbanded in January 1946 after almost six years of magnificent service.

Figure 7: Brancepeth Castle in 2015, Regimental Headquarters of the Durham Light Infantry during the Second World War.

Other Duties

Many Durham soldiers carried out numerous non-combat duties during the war. These were no less essential than the troops in North Africa, Italy and elsewhere. A good example of this was the garrison duties carried out in Iceland in 1940–1. Iceland was very important. Its location in the North Atlantic meant that ships and aircraft could be based there which would protect the merchant shipping from German U-boats and surface raiders. These ships carried vital supplies from the USA including food, weapons and ammunition and, later in the war, troops. Had the Germans got hold of Iceland, it would have been disastrous for the Allied war effort.

So Britain and Canada occupied Iceland in May 1940 and in September two battalions of the DLI arrived. Their main job was to protect Iceland from German invasion but they did lots of other work while they were there, including the construction of an aerodrome. Some of the Durhams had been at Dunkirk and so this was an ideal opportunity to recharge their batteries. The winter climate in Iceland was severe, icy cold and windy and often with poor quality snowbound roads. Some soldiers even had to take to skis. All trained hard and, when they left, they were well prepared for what lay ahead. The Icelanders themselves treated the British and Commonwealth troops warily at first. They were worried that, if the Germans arrived and threw the occupiers out, they might have been punished for collaborating with the Allies. When it became obvious that the Germans weren't coming, the locals began to treat the soldiers with warmth and friendship.

Back in England, Durham soldiers were busy carrying out all kinds of tasks. In the summer of 1940 many were involved with coastal and other defence against possible German invasion. Others carried out vital jobs such as protecting the railways, dockyards, ammunition depots and airfields. Some manned searchlights and anti-aircraft guns. Mobile units were formed to respond to threats such as landings from German paratroops. These were particularly needed during the 1940 invasion scare.

There were groups of DLI troops based in many populated areas of North East England: Newcastle, Sunderland, Gateshead, Durham, Bishop Auckland and Stockton-on-Tees. They were part of the national defence companies covering Northumberland, County Durham, Teesside and the North Yorkshire Coast.

In September 1939, Brancepeth Castle near Durham became the regimental headquarters of the Durham Light Infantry. The castle had been in a poor state for some time. There was no water, heating, lighting or electricity. At first all accommodation on site was in tents. These were eventually replaced with wooden huts. For a while troops were billeted in nearby villages: Willington, Meadowfield, Spennymoor and Esh Winning. One company was stationed in Durham City and others in Barnard Castle and Tow Law.

It took almost two years for Brancepeth Castle to become fully operational. Meanwhile, training continued wherever the troops were based. A huge range of important activities took place at the castle. Recruits underwent their basic training there. As the war proceeded, more and more young men were being enlisted all over the country. Few had any military experience. Good training was vital. Much of it in Durham was carried out by First World War veterans. Specific preparations for campaigns took place at Brancepeth, such as learning to master new weapons and tactics. Home Guard platoons and Army Cadet Force boys took part in training at regimental HQ.

The chief task at HQ was to turn out well-trained and fit soldiers. This they achieved with great distinction. Some who trained very hard were never needed overseas but carried out essential home-based duties instead. The Durham Light Infantry Training Centre at Brancepeth Castle had a national reputation for doing things properly. No wonder DLI troops made such a big contribution to the war effort.

Burma 1942–45

Often dubbed "the forgotten war", the battles in Burma between US, Chinese, British and Commonwealth, and Japanese troops were fought out in conditions as alien to the Allied forces as the North African desert had been. The Japanese had declared war by attacking the base of the US Pacific Fleet at Pearl Harbour in Hawaii in December 1941. They quickly followed this up by seizing the British stronghold of Singapore, the Philippines and large parts of present-day Indonesia. They were already practiced warriors, having been at war with China since the Japanese invaded Manchuria in 1931. They soon occupied most of Burma and began to threaten India, the jewel in the British Imperial crown.

Amongst the forces charged with first defending India from the Japanese and then driving them out of Burma were the 2nd Battalion of the Durham Light Infantry. The 2nd DLI had escaped from Dunkirk and returned to North East England. After a brief period of rest they resumed training and were brought up to strength through new recruits and soldiers returning following injury in France. Until the spring of 1942 they carried out home defence duties around Bridlington in East Yorkshire. In April 1942 they set sail for an unknown destination. Bombay (present-day Mumbai) was their port of call which they reached on 2 June 1942.

A period of intense training in jungle warfare and amphibious landings followed before they moved to Chittagong (in present-day Bangladesh) where they arrived on Christmas Day, 1942.

1943 was a disastrous year for the Allies in the Far East. Their soldiers were almost completely driven out of Burma and the Japanese expected to be carrying out a victory parade through the streets of the Indian capital, Delhi, at any time. They were far more accomplished jungle fighters and adapted to the heat, rain, dense jungle, hills, flies and disease much better than the Allies. The Durhams' first action saw them being part of a controlled retreat back to India at the battle of Indin. During the Japanese advance, the enemy were caught on open ground and slaughtered in their thousands. Meanwhile, the Chinese had joined the Burma war and they, together with the Americans, held the Japanese at bay for the rest of 1943.

The Durhams returned to Chittagong to undergo more jungle training. They were back in Burma in early 1944 to face another Japanese attempt to break through to India. Twice the Japanese tried to smash their way through the Allied defences and twice they failed. The enemy had put one hundred thousand troops into the field for this vital campaign. The fighting was very tough. The Japanese, who didn't recognise the word surrender, preferred the honour of death in battle. The Allied soldiers were constantly harassed by snipers.

The turning point came at the battle of Kohima where, after days of fierce fighting, the Japanese were defeated. It rained throughout the battle and the Durhams suffered many casualties and were very grateful to the Nagas, Burmese hill farmers, who acted as stretcher-bearers to carry the wounded soldiers away from the battlefield. When it was over, the DLI left a memorial:

When you go home
Tell them of us and say
For your tomorrow
We gave our today.

The Durhams then left for a well-earned rest and other regiments continued to push the enemy back. Two months later they were back at the front line and were amongst the troops who crossed the fiercely defended Irrawaddy River. This was the last great effort from the Japanese who, despite their fanaticism, were beaten back. They never recovered. Mandalay, Burma's second city, fell to the Allies at the end of March 1945. The last great obstacle before victory was the Burmese capital Rangoon (present-day Yangon). The Allied High Command decided to attack it from the sea so the Durhams were sent back to Calcutta (present-day Kolkata) for intense amphibious training.

By the time the attack was launched, the Japanese had gone. Those who had survived had returned to their homeland to defend it against the expected invasion by the USA. On 15 June the Allies marched in triumph through Rangoon. Less than two months later the war was over as the Japanese surrendered to the USA. In October 1945 the Durham Light Infantry sailed home.

Apart from a period in September 1943 when the 1st DLI got a bloody nose in trying to seize and hold an airfield on the Greek island of Kos, this completes the journey of the Durham Light Infantry with, of course, one major exception and this will be described in Chapter Five.

CHAPTER THREE

CAMPS
Nazi Concentration Camps 1933–1945

At Auschwitz, tell me, where was God?
William Styron, *Sophie's Choice*

Soldiers who fought in the Second World War, indeed any war, were usually well prepared to face anything that they might encounter on the battlefield. This was the result of intensive training before they went into battle. Soldiers knew how to handle weapons—many of them new, updated and more sophisticated during the Second World War—dig trenches, build bridges, drive many different forms of vehicle, live off the land, build roads, airfields and so on. They knew how to fight, they knew how to kill, and they knew how to survive.

The Durham Light Infantry were no exception. They'd received the best possible training (see Chapter Two) at Brancepeth. These were mostly young men, although, as the war proceeded, more men and women approaching middle age were called up. The men in civilian life had been shipyard workers, policemen, teachers and miners (there were few of these as the government eventually made coal mining a reserved occupation as the miners were thought to be too valuable at home doing their normal job). Joining them were bookkeepers, accountants, shop assistants, bus drivers, plumbers, joiners and folk from just about every walk of life. Some were professional soldiers who had enlisted before the war. Others had signed on in response to recruitment campaigns, a further group would have been conscripted and lastly there were the territorials, the part-time soldiers. All shared several things in common: they were fit, brave and ready to face up to the challenge of battle. But not one of them was ready to deal with the horrors that they faced in Northern Germany on 18 April 1945.

What the DLI and other troops faced on that day was a concentration camp. These dreadful places will forever be associated with Nazi Germany but they were in use as long ago as Roman times. The forerunners of the modern camps were those used by the United States government to control the movement of Cherokee Native Americans in the early nineteenth century. Towards the end of that century, the Spanish used them in Cuba and the British against the families of the Boer farmers in the Second South African war (see Chapter One). The British have the dubious distinction of coining the phrase "concentration camp". There were a number of factors common to all concentration camps:

- The detainees were usually arrested and sent to the camps without trial.
- The camps were makeshift rather than purpose built, often compounds with huts surrounded by barbed wire.
- The detainees had no idea as to how long they would be detained.
- The detainees usually comprised groups of people opposed to the government which was imprisoning them. These people were concentrated in one place.
- Groups of people might be imprisoned because of membership of a political party, race/colour, sexual orientation, religious beliefs or employment status.

The Nazis will always be remembered for their concentration camps and, in particular, for the killing of millions of Jews who were imprisoned there. But they didn't start out with that purpose.

In January of 1933 Adolf Hitler became Chancellor of Germany. He gained this position by perfectly legitimate means. Strictly speaking, Hitler answered to the President, an old soldier called Hindenburg. In practice, the President was too old and frail to stand up to Hitler, who proceeded to rule Germany, along with his Nazi party comrades, much as he pleased.

Germany, in common with many other countries in the 1920s and 1930s, was in the grip of an economic depression. Unemployment was high and wages were low. These circumstances created a fertile breeding ground for extreme political parties like the communists and the Nazis. The Nazis, like the Italian government, were fascists and their chief political opponents were the communists. Communism was stronger in Germany than anywhere else outside the Soviet Union (Russia). Hitler knew that he had to get rid of it.

Less than a month after Hitler became Chancellor, there was an arson attack on the Reichstag (German parliament). A man was arrested. The blame was placed on the communists. Hitler acted quickly and ordered that all known communists be arrested and locked up in all kinds of buildings like disused factories and warehouses, old farms, cellars, anywhere where they could be held in "protective custody". The arrests were carried out not by the police but by the Sturmabteilung (SA or Brownshirts), a paramilitary bunch of thugs who'd done Hitler's dirty work for him in the street battles with the communists in the late nineteen twenties and early thirties. The prisoners were beaten, tortured and forced to reveal the names of their comrades. The pattern for the concentration camps was set and about 100,000 known opponents of the Nazis were locked up in the spring and summer of 1933. During the course of the communist round-ups, it became obvious that current prisons and the SA's disparate collection of buildings couldn't cope with the new influx. As a result the first of the "purpose built" camps opened at Oranienburg (replaced by Sachsenhausen in 1936) near Berlin and this was quickly followed in March 1933 by Dachau, near Munich, one of the most infamous of all.

The Nazis didn't hide the existence of the camps and paraded them in the newspapers as centres of re-education. The press were allowed to see what went on inside the camps. So successful was this *re-education* programme that most communists imprisoned earlier in the year were released by Christmas 1933 after promising never again to engage in political activity.

Hitler had said in his autobiographical work *Mein Kampf* that he would use camps to imprison his opponents without trial and now he began to deliver on his promise. At first the camps were staffed and run by the SA but soon Hitler handed control to his own private army, the Schutzstaffel (SS). These black-uniformed engineers of terror set a pattern at Dachau that was to grow into the greatest network of state-sponsored evil the world has ever seen At first, their idea of torture was the unrestricted use of fists, boots and whips. Any inmate found guilty of political agitation was hanged without trial. Two months after the SS took over the running of Dachau twelve inmates had been murdered, including four "trying to escape". Occasionally in these early days of the Third Reich, guards were arrested and charged in state courts with unnecessary brutality but this soon stopped as the Nazi grip on Germany strengthened. Those charged who were found guilty received very lenient sentences.

As the camps were slowly emptied of "re-educated" communists, so other groups of people of whom the Nazis were afraid took their place:

- Trade Unionists
- Social Democrats
- Socialists
- Those working in film, radio and the written media
- Ministers of some churches

Figure 8: A cremation oven at Bergen-Belsen (photo: The RAMC Muniment Collection in the care of the Wellcome Library; Wellcome Images, no. L0029088).

At least two very senior pastors who had voiced opposition to Hitler were sent to the camps. Doctor Wissler of the Confessional Church was murdered at Sachsenhausen in 1936 and Doctor Neimoeller was arrested in July 1937 and ended up at Dachau where he stayed throughout the war until it was liberated by US troops in April 1945.

The SS, under the leadership of Heinrich Himmler, were now in charge of the camps. Hitler became convinced that the SA were becoming so powerful that even his own position might be threatened. On 30 June 1934, he initiated a purge against the SA. Many of the Brownshirts were dragged out of their beds and shot and others were taken to prison and shot. The SA Leader Ernst Röhm was marched off to prison where, on 2 July, he too was shot. Standing up to Röhm's thugs increased Hitler's prestige, both in the nation as a whole and particularly in the German army whose support he would need in the years to come.

The much weakened SA continued to exist and would have their uses to Hitler in the future but the "Night of the Long Knives", as the purge became known, enabled the SS to establish themselves as the predominant police and paramilitary force in Nazi Germany. Two years later the camp at Sachsenhausen was opened, followed a year later by Buchenwald in East Central Germany, about one hundred miles west of Dresden. In 1938, the Nazis moved into Austria and incorporated that country into Germany. The Austrian Chancellor Schuschnigg was arrested and sent to Dachau where he remained until the Americans arrived in the spring of 1945. During the war Hitler regularly sacked Wehrmacht generals. Some were sent to concentration camps. Franz Halder, dismissed in 1942, spent the rest of the war at Dachau and was also rescued by the Americans in April 1945. An Austrian concentration camp was quickly built at Mauthausen near Linz. Excluding the later extermination camps, more prisoners died at Mauthausen than at any other camp. Mauthausen was built adjacent to a quarry and prisoners were forced to carry huge lumps of rock on their backs. When they fell over with exhaustion, they were shot. Over thirty-five thousand died in this way. Included in this total were forty-seven Allied bomber crew who were murdered in retaliation for raids on German towns and cities. Later that year a camp at Flossenburg in Bavaria was opened. Women prisoners were first accommodated at Lichtenburg, a renaissance castle in Saxony, but, when this closed in 1939, it was replaced by Ravensbrück, a camp exclusively for women detainees, which opened in May 1939. Together with Dachau this completed the Nazis' pre-war concentration camp programme in Germany and Austria.

Sub-camps sprung up near to these, mostly to house slave labourers who mined the quarries to provide the materials for Germany's ambitious building programme. The best known of these construction projects was the autobahn (motorway) network and the new Reich Chancellery in Berlin. Others worked in factories helping with the production of essential items for the waging of war.

Before the autumn of 1938, Jews in the concentration camps were in the minority. If they were there it was often for a reason other than their religion. A substantial number of Jews were communists, for example. People who were imprisoned in the camps had to wear an upside-down fabric triangle sewn on to their uniforms as a badge of shame, colour-coded to indicate why they were there:

- **Black:** Vagrants, beggars, work-shy
- **Blue:** Returning Jewish emigrants
- **Red:** Political prisoners
- **Violet:** Jehovah's Witnesses
- **Pink:** Homosexuals
- **Brown:** Gypsies
- **Green:** Professional criminals
- **Red (un-inverted):** Spies, army deserters

Jewish prisoners imprisoned in any of the above categories had to wear an additional badge: the yellow star of David.

Beggars and unemployed people were favourite targets. Ten thousand were arrested and sent to camps in the summer of 1938. Sometimes, others convicted by the state courts and sentenced to a term of imprisonment were re-arrested on their release and taken to a concentration camp.

Inside the camps the prisoners were treated brutally, the food was of a very poor quality and low in quantity, the sanitary arrangements totally disgusting and the provision for sleeping completely inadequate. Most of the SS guards were unpleasant men and women of very low intelligence. Delivering beatings and torture gave them a sense of self-importance that they wouldn't have been able to gain outside the camps. The SS completely controlled every aspect of camp life from the commandant, through the officers and guards, down to the cooks. Many of the commandants had cut their teeth at Dachau, the academy of evil. Deaths from disease and malnutrition were commonplace. There were some executions, usually carried out after a camp court, consisting entirely of SS personnel, had passed a death sentence, which was normally carried out by hanging. Many inmates died of exhaustion after days and months of back-breaking work in the quarries. The camp perimeters were patrolled by Alsatians, Dobermans and Boxers. Inside, the prisoners had no idea when, if ever, they'd be released. Political prisoners were often forced to learn and sing Nazi songs as part of their "re-education" programme.

From the very beginning of the Third Reich, the Jews were persecuted by the Nazis. In April 1933 there was a one-day boycott of Jewish shops. The anti-Semitic (anti-Jewish) measures increased as the Nazis forced their political enemies into prisons, camps or exile. Jewish people were thrown out of their jobs, made to sell their businesses at ridiculously low prices and Jewish children were barred from attending German schools. German doctors and dentists were forbidden to treat Jewish patients and Jewish teachers, university professors and lawyers were sacked. Before the war, the Nazi plan was to get rid of their Jews, not by killing them but by forcing them to emigrate. A series of laws was passed in 1935 (the Nuremberg Laws) which defined what the Nazis considered Aryan (of pure German and Northern European blood). People who had three or four Jewish grandparents were classified as non-Aryan and these people had their German citizenship revoked. They were now called subjects. Marriage and sexual relationships between Aryans and non-Aryans were banned.

By the start of the war, half of Germany's 1933 total of one million Jews had left the country. They went to other Western European countries, the USA, some to Palestine and others to Eastern Europe. At this stage, the concentration camps had not been much used to detain the Jews but this all changed on the night of 9–10 November 1938. On this night, there was a well-planned series of pogroms (attacks) on Jews throughout Germany and Austria. The pretext was the assassination of a German diplomat in Paris by a young Polish Jew. Given the green light by Hitler and organised by Himmler and Josef Goebbels (Minister of Propaganda), Brownshirts (not in uniform) attacked Jews and their property throughout the two countries. Synagogues were burned, Jewish shops smashed to pieces and Jewish homes and property desecrated. Some Jewish men had their beards set on fire and many Jews were kicked and beaten by the SA, who were responsible for ninety-one murders. Ordinary Germans stood by and watched in horror. Over one thousand synagogues and seven thousand businesses were destroyed. Jewish hospitals and schools were attacked and thirty thousand men were arrested and marched off to their nearest concentration camp. The pogrom became known as *Kristallnacht* ("Night of the Broken Glass"). Most of those imprisoned were soon released from the camps but some were kept in and, as war approached, more and more Jews were imprisoned in the camps. A significant number of the twenty-one thousand incarcerated in camps at the start of the war were Jewish.

At the outbreak of war there were nine million Jews in Europe (including half a million in Germany). When it was over there were just three million. As soon as the Germans invaded Poland they started killing Jewish civilians. As the German Army (Wehrmacht) swept all before them, so they were followed by mobile death squads (Einsatzgruppen) whose instructions were to kill all the Jews and Polish intellectuals they could find. The intelligentsia were targeted because they were regarded as a potential source of resistance to the German invaders. This pattern was repeated when the Germans invaded the Soviet Union in 1941. As the Wehrmacht carried all before it on the roads to Moscow and Leningrad, so the mobile killing units followed them and carried out their ghastly tasks. The Einsatzgruppen were responsible for two of the war's most infamous mass killings. At Babi Yar in Ukraine over thirty thousand men, women and children were shot and then buried in mass graves in September 1941. Two months later at Rumbula in Latvia twenty-five thousand Jewish people were murdered in the same way. At the end of the war it was estimated that the Einsatzgruppen were responsible for killing more than three million civilians, including over one million Jews.

This method of killing was straightforward enough in the villages where the Jews and other racial groups amongst the population who were hated by the Nazis were taken from their homes and shot, but it was more difficult in the larger towns and cities where there were fewer places to hide the corpses and too many witnesses. So the Nazi administration decided to herd all Jews into a small part of each town and surrounded the area with barbed wire. Families were forced into sharing houses. Sometimes ten or more families shared a tenement building designed for three or four. Food was scarce and sanitation appalling. Many of the Jewish families who lived in these hellholes died of either malnutrition or disease or worked as slave labourers. The largest of these ghettos were in the Jewish cities of Warsaw, Lodz and Lvov (now Lviv in present-day Ukraine). These wired-in communities served as holding camps while the Nazis decided what to do with the Jews.

The answer, of course, was to build concentration camps, predominantly in Poland, although there were also sites in Estonia, Latvia, Lithuania, Czechoslovakia (modern-day Czech Republic and Slovakia), Hungary, Yugoslavia (modern-day Croatia and Serbia), Norway and Ukraine. Initially, these were constructed to house prisoners-of-war, political enemies, Jews, gypsies and other racial and religious groups despised by the Nazis. Their main purpose was to supply a ready source of slave labour. The site for one of the largest camps, Auschwitz in Southern Poland, was opened in May 1940. The first arrivals were Polish political prisoners. The site, which had been an army barracks in the past, was to be used to house a synthetic rubber and coal oil plant managed by the German industrial giant IG Farben. The prisoners first built and then later operated this plant. The Germans were, at first, more concerned with using prisoners to act as slave labour for the war effort and Auschwitz, like many other camps, grew into a vast enterprise, embracing several parts of the main camps and several sub-camps.

Until 1941, the killing of Europe's Jews was a horribly haphazard business. It was mostly carried out by shooting or burning people in barns. It was also too slow for the Nazis' liking. Senior SS officers met at Wannsee, a district of Berlin, in 1942 and decided to round up all of the remaining European Jews and kill them.

The Wannsee Conference decided on the "final solution to the Jewish question". Until this time the camps were either:

- Prisoner-of-war camps
- Forced labour camps
- Concentration camps

Now two new categories were added:

- Transit camps
- Extermination camps

Transit camps were to house prisoners until such time as they could be transferred to an extermination camp. Two of the best known of these were Westerbork in the Netherlands and Drancy in France. Labour camps became increasingly important as the war proceeded. More and more young German men were being called up to fight and it was important to replace them on factory floors, especially in the armaments industry. If you were a Jew and sent to a death camp, your greatest chance of survival was if you were young or middle-aged and in reasonable health. Or, in other words, fit to work. Signs of exhaustion meant certain death.

Jews from every country in German-occupied Europe were rounded up by the SS, sometimes helped by local policemen in the occupied countries, and sent to the death camps. The vast majority of these camps were in Poland, out of sight of ordinary Germans. Chief amongst them were:

- Auschwitz-Birkenau
- Belzec
- Janowska
- Majdanek
- Sobibor
- Treblinka

The prisoners had to endure long journeys by train across several countries before they reached their destinations. They were transported in cattle trucks in the most inhumane conditions, often with little room to lie down. Not surprisingly, many died during the journey. On arrival at their destinations, most of the prisoners were gassed and their corpses burned. The exceptions to this were older teenagers and adults in reasonable health who were thought to be fit enough to work. When their strength left them after weeks and months of hard labour, they too were murdered. Lilly Ebert, prisoner number 10572, was fourteen when she was sent to Auschwitz from Hungary with her mother, brother and three sisters. In 2010 she told the London Evening Standard's Ross Lydall of her arrival at Auschwitz.

> When we came out of the shower, our hair was cut and our belongings taken away. They left us with only our shoes. We saw a fire in the chimneys, and a terrible smell.
>
> We asked people who were already there. They told us it was not a factory. They said it was our parents and brothers and sisters who were being burned.
>
> **London Evening Standard,** *26 January 2010*

Before they were killed, the condemned were forced to undress and taken into what appeared to be a shower room but was, in fact, an enormous gas chamber. When they were all inside, the doors were locked and sealed and poisonous hydrogen cyanide pellets were dropped through the air vents. Everyone was dead within thirty minutes. The poisonous air was pumped out and other Jewish prisoners, wearing gas masks, first checked the corpses for gold teeth fillings and rings. Then the murdered Jews were loaded onto wagons and taken to a nearby furnace where they were burned.

Sometimes the ashes of the dead were used for fertiliser. Any gold, including teeth, was subsequently melted down and made into gold bars.

The first extermination camp was at Belzec in the south-east corner of Poland. It became operational in March 1942. By the time it was closed in June 1943, four hundred and thirty thousand had been gassed. The camp was conveniently located close to a railway line, as were all of the Polish camps. The organisation of what became known as the Holocaust fell into the hands of SS Colonel Adolf Eichmann. He escaped to Argentina after the war and made a new home for himself and his family in Buenos Aires. In 1960 he was kidnapped by a small team of Israeli secret service agents, smuggled out of South America and taken to Israel. He was tried for war crimes in Jerusalem, found guilty, and hanged in 1962.

Auschwitz was the most horribly efficient of the extermination camps. At its peak the SS were killing six thousand people a day. It was part of a large complex of camps:

- **Auschwitz I:** concentration camp
- **Auschwitz II (Birkenau):** extermination camp
- **Auschwitz III:** forced labour camp

There were also further sub-camps in the region. As the war turned against the Germans, the Nazis set up more and more forced labour camps in an attempt to keep their war effort going. So desperate were they for labour that they kept prisoners alive for as long as possible. Without this necessity, many more would have been murdered. A typical example of a forced labour camp was Plaszow near Krakow. The commandant was Amon Goeth, played chillingly well by Ralph Fiennes in Steven Spielberg's Holocaust masterpiece *Schindler's List*. At the end of the war, Goeth was hanged by the Russians.

Almost three of the six million victims of the Holocaust died in the Polish extermination camps. Most of them were Jews.

- **Auschwitz-Birkenau:**   1.1 million
- **Belzec:**   434,000
- **Janowska:**   40,000
- **Majdanek:**   78,000
- **Sobibor:**   200,000
- **Treblinka:**   870,000

After the war ended, the full horror of what went on in these camps was revealed. A number of SS men and women in all of the camps, not just the extermination camps, carried out monstrous medical experiments on the prisoners. Many are far too gruesome to be described here but these examples will give some indication of the cruelty of the Nazis:

Figure 9: The entrance gate to the Auschwitz-Birkenau extermination camp (photo: C. Puisney).

- Finding out how long prisoners could survive drinking only salt water
- Injecting lethal diseases like typhus into prisoners
- Sterilisation experiments
- Immersing prisoners in tanks of icy water until they froze to death
- Leaving prisoners naked outside in sub-zero temperatures until they froze to death

The purpose of these experiments, apart from the sadistic pleasure they gave to the SS overseers, was to learn lessons that might benefit German soldiers, sailors and airmen in extreme conditions.

It has never been clear just how much Hitler knew about the horrors of the extermination camps. Whether he knew or not doesn't stop him from being fully accountable for the Holocaust. It was his fanatical hatred of the Jews that encouraged his fawning followers to organise and perform these appalling crimes. Had he survived the war, Hitler would certainly have ended up on the gallows alongside many of his sycophantic subjects.

By the winter of 1944, the Soviet Union's Red Army was driving the Germans out of Poland. One by one, the camps were liberated but not at Auschwitz where the SS decided to move all of the surviving prisoners back to the relative safety of Germany where any who made it alive would be put to work. Some were forced to march barefoot across central Europe in freezing conditions. Those who fell were shot. Groups showing signs of weakness were herded into barns and burnt to death. Those who made it found themselves in German concentration camps, chief amongst them the North German camp at Bergen-Belsen.

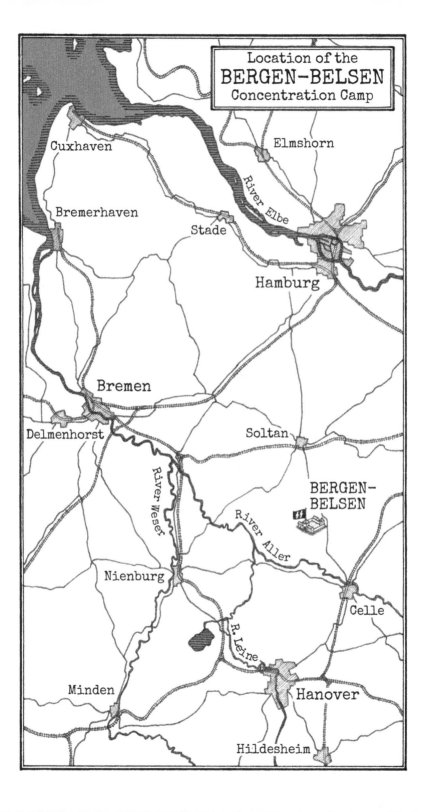

Location of the
BERGEN-BELSEN
Concentration Camp

Cuxhaven
Elmshorn
River Elbe
Bremerhaven
Stade
Hamburg
Bremen
Delmenhorst
Soltan
River Weser
BERGEN-BELSEN
River Aller
Nienburg
Celle
R. Leine
Minden
Hanover
Hildesheim

BELSEN

1936–1945

Death has moved in to stay.
Hanna Lévy-Hass, *Diary of Bergen-Belsen 1944–1945*

The Bergen-Belsen concentration camp was located in Northern Germany. Today, the nearest large town to the site is Celle and the best-known big city nearby is Hannover, just under forty miles to the south. Hamburg is a little further away to the north.

The whole area surrounding Belsen was flat and densely forested, ideal for military training, and that is how this part of Lower Saxony began life: as a training area for the Wehrmacht (German military personnel) in 1935.

Although the Nazis had shown few outward signs of preparing for war before 1936, re-militarising the Rhineland (including Cologne) signalled a change to that. The Germans had been forbidden to station soldiers in that area after their defeat in the Great War (1914–1918) to protect the neighbouring countries of France, Belgium and Luxembourg from future invasion. Ignoring this, soldiers were sent into the Rhineland in March 1936. The Treaty of Versailles (1919) had forbidden this and the building of an air force, as well as restricting the size of the German army, preventing their union with Austria and other measures. This was Adolf Hitler's first aggressive step in foreign policy since he had established himself as the undisputed leader of the Third Reich.

The reoccupation of the Rhineland saw the start of German preparations for war, which followed three and a half years later. In 1936 a number of huts were erected to house the three thousand workers who were building a military barracks nearby, where the main purpose was to train crews for military vehicles, tanks, half-tracks and so on. The workers left in 1939 and the huts remained empty until the spring and summer of 1940, when they became the Stalag XI prisoner-of-war camp. Six hundred French and Belgian soldiers were held there following the defeat of those countries in the huge German spring offensive of May and June.

Over the course of the next twelve months, these prisoners were mostly sent elsewhere, either back to their own countries or shipped to labour camps in other parts of Germany. In June 1941, Germany, without warning, invaded the Soviet Union. As in Belgium, Luxembourg, the Netherlands and France twelve months earlier, the Wehrmacht carried all before them. Tens of thousands of prisoners quickly fell into their hands. Twenty thousand of these were sent to Belsen. Immediately the camp became horribly overcrowded. Many Russians were forced to sleep in the open, either in ditches or else on open ground covered in branches. Later, tents were provided and new huts were built, but it was too late for these poor men, two-thirds of whom died of cold, starvation and disease within a year. Only the Jews incurred greater hatred from Hitler than the millions of Slavic people who populated vast areas of Eastern Europe, including the Soviet Union. Consequently the camp guards did nothing to try to keep the Russians alive. Their treatment was appalling, in direct contrast to that of British prisoners of war who, by and large, were looked after reasonably well.

The function of Belsen changed once more in April 1943, when the head of the SS, Heinrich Himmler, turned it into a concentration camp under SS control. Fences and watchtowers were built and the guards were heavily armed. It would be virtually impossible to escape. Soon thousands of Jewish men, women and children were sent there alongside gypsies, homosexuals, Jehovah's Witnesses, anti-Nazi Christians, other political prisoners and common criminals. There were several camps, the largest of which was divided into smaller camps:

- Men's camp
- Women's camp
- Camp for Jewish refugees
- Camp for other Jewish people
- Neutral camp for criminals, political prisoners etc.

There was also a forced labour camp providing bodies to work in a factory reconstituting leather from old shoes. These shoes may have belonged to Jews who had died in the Polish camps. Some Jewish hostages were a special category of inmate whom the Germans planned to release in exchange for their own personnel captured by the enemy. Many of the *exchange Jews* had passports for South American countries or visas to enter Palestine. Of the thousands held as hostages, several hundred were sent to neutral Switzerland and just over two hundred emigrated to Palestine. Until the last months of 1944, Belsen was also used as a transit camp for those who were later transferred to the death camps in the east where, inevitably, they were killed.

It was in the final months of 1944 that the tragedy of Belsen began to unfold. More huts had been built but there were nothing like enough to accommodate the camp's population which had grown from fifteen thousand towards the end of 1944 to over forty thousand by the beginning of the following March. The Red Army (Russians) were relentlessly driving the Germans out of Eastern Europe and back to their own borders. As they did, they began to reach the Nazi death camps in Poland. The Germans had tried to hide the evidence by wiping out all traces of some (e.g. Treblinka) and by blowing up gas chambers and evacuating prisoners in others (e.g. Auschwitz). Tens of thousands of largely Jewish prisoners were forced to march westwards in the height of winter. Some had to walk without shoes on the frozen and snow-covered ground. Those who fell or stumbled were immediately shot by the SS guards who periodically arranged mass burnings in barns. Hardly anyone was left in Auschwitz when the Russians arrived in January 1945. Survivors had already set off on their "death march" to the west. Amongst their destinations was Belsen and it was amazing that anyone made it there alive. But they did, and in their thousands.

Amongst these survivors was Anne Frank, a fifteen-year-old German Jewish girl whose parents had taken their family to live in Amsterdam when Hitler came to power in 1933. After the Germans defeated the Dutch in 1940, the SS began their hunt for Dutch Jews. Anne and other members of her family hid in a tiny space in a house in Amsterdam until they were betrayed and sent to Auschwitz in 1943. Anne Frank's account of her years in hiding, *The Diary of a Young Girl*, is a classic of Holocaust literature and was filmed in 1959. The house in which she lived is now a museum.

Belsen was not an extermination camp. No evidence has been found of gas chambers but there was a crematorium where the corpses of those who died of hunger, disease and ill-treatment by the guards were destroyed.

As the final year of the Second World War began, a disaster of unimaginable proportions was unfolding at Belsen. Every week thousands of new prisoners arrived, adding to the already chronic overcrowding. The SS made some feeble attempts to deal with this. Some new huts were built by slave labourers. The bunks were three-tiered and the prisoners slept at least three to a bed. Tents were used for some of the new arrivals who had to endure days and nights of the windswept cold climate. None of this so-called indoor accommodation came close to providing adequate protection against the weather. When it rained, the floors of the huts became deep in mud and rats and mice were everywhere. Some huts, built to house one hundred people, had as many as six hundred in them. The food was atrocious, usually consisting of a thin cup of coffee made from acorns, one slice of bread each morning and evening and some watery soup with turnips, usually used to feed pigs, at lunchtime. The sanitation arrangements were dreadful. The washing facilities were outdoors in the open air and consisted only of cold water. The toilets consisted of long trenches where inmates had to carry out their natural bodily functions in full view of their fellow prisoners. Bizarrely, the International Red Cross paid an inspection visit in December 1944. Their job was to ensure that prisoners were kept in humane conditions. Under threat of death from the SS, the inmates toiled away to get Belsen fit for the visitors. Everything, buildings, huts, washrooms and so on were scrubbed. The dead and dying were hidden. The guards smiled at the inmates throughout the visit and, before they left, the Red Cross handed out chocolates to the prisoners. In the same month an indescribably bad situation became worse when Josef Kramer was appointed the new commandant. He had been transferred from Auschwitz where he had been in charge of the gas chambers. He immediately instituted an even harsher regime, encouraging guards to physically and verbally abuse the prisoners and ordering roll-calls of up to five hours with the prisoners standing in the worst of weathers. Food rations were stopped for even the slightest reason. Prisoners were forced to crawl on their knees while being whipped by the guards. Kramer soon earned the nickname "the beast of Belsen" and kept up the persecution by scrapping the evening bread ration. Kramer gave greater power to the favoured German prisoners in charge of the huts (kapos) who behaved even more barbarically than the guards in order to impress the SS. In his spare time, Kramer amused himself by taking pot shots at prisoners scrambling for food. As rumours of Germany's collapse spread amongst the inmates and the SS, the guards became even more brutal and anarchy began to rear its head amongst the prisoners themselves.

> Our barracks are an insane asylum. Rare are those who know how to control themselves. The slightest incident gives rise to violent quarrels, insults, threats. Everybody has become extremely touchy, always ready to lose their temper and see others as their personal enemy. Distrust, suspicion and ill have entered every heart; it makes you shudder.
>
> *Hanna Lévy-Hass,* **Diary of Bergen-Belsen***, 1944–1945*

The SS women guards were hardly any better. The most notorious of them was Irma Grese who had tried, unsuccessfully, in 1942, to become a nurse but was sent instead to the Ravensbrück concentration camp in Germany. Here she built a reputation as an unremittingly cruel guard. So greatly did her acts of cruelty find favour with her superiors she was promoted and sent to Auschwitz where she was the second highest ranking female member of the SS personnel, despite being only nineteen years old at the time. After the closure of Auschwitz she returned briefly to Ravensbrück before being sent to Belsen.

Like all members of the SS, Grese was always immaculately dressed, in pressed uniform, shining boots, painted nails and beautifully groomed hair. She carried a whip and pistol, shot men, women and children in cold blood, whipped inmates and kicked them into unconsciousness before setting half-starved dogs on to them. Her inhuman behaviour earned her the nickname amongst the residents of the *beautiful beast* to add to the one she had earned in one of her previous places of employment, *the hyena of Auschwitz*.

Tomi Reichental was just nine when he was sent to Belsen. He remembers Irma Grese.

> She walked about in heavy boots and carried both a pistol and a whip, and all three items—boots, pistol and whip— were wilfully inflicted on human beings who crossed her in some little way. She shot men, women and children in cold blood, whipped inmates until they were bloody and torn on the ground, when she would kick them about the head until they lost consciousness or died, whichever happened first.
>
> **Tomi Reichental, I was a Boy in Belsen**

In February 1945, the Red Army were advancing on Germany from the east and the remaining allies were making similarly spectacular progress from the west. The war was lost for Germany. Many of those inside Belsen knew this but their suffering continued. They tried their best to improve their circumstances, even conducting lessons for the children, despite this being forbidden by the Germans. Occasionally there were parties like, for example, when the Dutch Jews celebrated their Queen's birthday.

Mostly it was a tale of never-ending horror. Pregnant women gave birth to stillborn infants whose tiny bodies were then thrown into the latrine trenches. SS guards even looted corpses, although what they found it's hard to imagine. Illness was everywhere then, when it seemed things could get no worse, typhus broke out in March 1945.

Typhus in the 1940s was a killer disease especially in places where sanitation, food and living conditions were of an appallingly low standard. It was caused by rats carrying fleas and by lice being transferred from one person to another. The symptoms included stomach, back, muscle and joint pain, headaches, rashes, high temperature up to 106 degrees Fahrenheit, vomiting and diarrhoea. The dreadful conditions at Belsen in the winter of 1945 made a fertile ground in which typhus could flourish. There was a disinfection facility at the camp but this broke down almost as soon as the epidemic began. The water supply was constantly interrupted by Allied air raids. The pilots, presumably, had no idea they were attacking a concentration camp but more likely thought that the whole area was a barracks and training area for the Wehrmacht which, of course, it was.

People started dying soon after the start of the outbreak. There was no medicine, hardly any food and hopelessly inadequate sanitation. So many were dying, it became impossible to dispose of the corpses. The crematorium couldn't cope, the mass graves were full and so bodies were dumped outside the huts. The kapos ordered the healthier prisoners to carry the bodies from the huts. Often people found the person next to them had died during the sleepless nights. Inside the huts, lives descended into hell.

> I look at the gloomy barracks full of ghosts, humiliation, hatred, these motionless sick people reduced to total powerlessness, these living and already putrefied corpses, a dark abyss where an entire humanity founders.
>
> *Hanna Lévy-Hass,* **Diary of Bergen-Belsen, 1944–1945**

The sick prisoners' bodies crawled with lice and some spent days picking the insects off each other. It became almost impossible to sleep as screams of agony resonated through the huts at night. Suicides happened regularly. The prisoners' favourite method was to make a run for the barbed wire fences which enclosed the camp, hoping to get shot by the guards in the watch towers. Every morning corpses were found entangled in the wire or lying at the foot of it. Yet still new prisoners arrived as the camps in the east were evacuated. There were forty thousand extra inmates in March alone. Some attempt was made to evacuate the hostage Jews by train. Many died but some were rescued by Allied soldiers.

As the Third Reich continued to collapse, the distribution of food broke down and from the end of March supplies stopped altogether. The SS guards, terrified that they would catch typhus, began to vanish in the middle of March, leaving the brutal kapos in charge. Kramer remained in the military barracks nearby. The death toll mounted. Eighteen thousand died in March including, at the end of the month, Anne Frank. Some prisoners began to lose their sanity and there were rumours of cannibalism. Kramer tried, unsuccessfully, to find food. On 10 April he met with fellow SS officer Kurt Becher and they decided that the only way to halt the deaths in the camp and prevent the disease spreading to the outside world was to ask the advancing British Army to take responsibility for Belsen. Fortunately the two SS officers ignored Himmler's orders to kill all the prisoners and abandon the camp. On 15 April 1945, an advance party of soldiers approached the camp. They had absolutely no knowledge of what they would find there.

CHAPTER FIVE

CAMPAIGNS
The Durham Light Infantry in
Western Europe, 1944–1945

We sure liberated the hell out of this place.
**American soldier comment on the ruins
of a village in Normandy, 1944**

When the Durham soldiers waded on to Gold Beach in Normandy on 6 June 1944, the Second World War had just ten months to run. Countless battles had been fought on land and sea and in the air for almost five years. Millions of lives had been lost and yet the worst of the war was still to come: the great battles of both the Eastern and Western fronts, the awful revelations about the German concentration camps, the first use of nuclear weapons in warfare and the displacement of millions of people who had lost their homes and, in many cases, their countries.

That Germany was going to lose the war was in no doubt from the middle of 1943. Her forces had been driven out of North Africa, they were fighting a desperate rear guard action in Italy, their U boats (submarines) were at last losing the battle of the Atlantic and they had suffered a calamitous defeat to the Red Army at Kursk, in Russia, where almost one million Germans had lined up against twice that number of Russians. The Russians also had almost double the number of tanks and one and a half times the number of heavy field guns. The Germans had struck first in a campaign which lasted a week and a half in July 1943, and the Soviet counter-attack lasted over a month. At the end, the Germans had been decisively defeated after the greatest armoured clash in history. More than a quarter of a million Germans were killed, injured or taken prisoner. Nearly one thousand tanks and assault weapons had been destroyed as well as over eight hundred aircraft. The losses on the Soviet side were even greater, almost one million men and thousands of tanks and artillery. The Russians who had started the battle with a huge superiority in men and machines struck a blow against the Third Reich from which it would never recover.

The Russians had already lost millions of men in the war and their leader Josef Stalin was putting pressure on the allies to open up a second front in the west. This became *Operation Overlord* and was characterised by the greatest seaborne invasion in history. Planning had begun in the middle of 1943. The landings were to take place on the beaches of Northern France. Agents who the Germans believed were spying for them but were, in fact, double agents working for the Allies, fed information back to the German High Command suggesting that it was likely that the invasion would come via the Pas de Calais. The Allies even assembled a large dummy invasion force of wooden aeroplanes and inflatable tanks in South East England. There was even an actual General based there, the American George Patton, to give more credibility to the deception which was known as *Plan Fortitude*. A similar force was put together in Scotland, making the Germans think that the invasion might come through Norway. The result was that the Germans kept troops and equipment in two areas where they weren't required. Had they been certain that the landings on 6 June 1944 (D-Day) were to take place in Normandy, they would have poured more troops into North West France and a difficult task might well have become impossible. Even after the 6 June landings, the operators of *Plan Fortitude* continued to send intelligence to the Wehrmacht that the Normandy attacks were just a feint and that the real targets were further east. This, vitally, delayed the German response. All of this is brilliantly described by Ben Macintyre in his book *Double Cross: The True Story of the D-Day Spies.*

A huge assault force, comprising men, tanks, artillery, landing craft, fighter and bomber planes, was assembled in the south of England. Five beaches were chosen for the initial assault:

- Utah Beach on the Cherbourg Peninsular where the Americans landed was the most westerly of the landing sites.
- Omaha Beach, another where the US troops landed, proved to be the toughest nut to crack. The US invasion force had sailed mostly from Cornwall, Devon and Dorset.
- Gold Beach, predominantly British troops who had sailed from Southampton.
- Juno Beach, mostly Canadian soldiers who had sailed from Portsmouth.
- Sword Beach was the most easterly of the sites. A combined force of British and Free French soldiers had sailed from Newhaven.

Soldiers who had escaped from German invasion of their countries such as Poland, Czechoslovakia, Greece, the Netherlands and Belgium earlier in the war fought alongside the Allies as well as troops from other Commonwealth countries including Australia, New Zealand and India.

The 6th, 8th and 9th Battalions of the Durham Light Infantry had returned to England from Sicily in August 1943. Chapter Two told the story of how they had carried out successful landings on the Sicilian beaches and played a significant part, along with other

Allied troops, in driving the Germans off that island. They might
have expected to take part in the next step, the invasion of Italy, but
instead, after a brief period of rest, they found themselves in Suffolk
(November 1943). Having fought in very tough campaigns in North
Africa and Sicily, they were slightly disappointed to discover that
they were to be amongst the first to land in German occupied France
as part of *Operation Overlord*. This wasn't a question of cowardice.
They were simply worn out. However, they quickly came to realise
that their selection was a compliment. Montgomery paid them a
visit in February 1944 and told them that their experience in other
theatres of war was vital and that they were a totally reliable unit
of fighting men.

Training in Suffolk was intense. There were new battle techniques
to be learned and new weapons to master. In April 1944, the
Durhams moved to Romsey in Hampshire. Here a huge security
blanket was thrown over the camps. Visitors were not allowed and
the troops were forbidden to divulge their location in letters home.

The date for the invasion was fixed for 4 June. However, the
weather turned stormy at the last moment and there was a twenty-
four-hour postponement. A day later conditions had improved
and the crossings went ahead although many of the sailors were
sick, unused to the rough seas. Before the ground invasion force
set sail, bombers of both the RAF and US Air Force pounded the
German positions behind the beaches. Then came the paratroopers
and, finally, the glider-mounted attacks. Both these groups had
the objectives of securing important communication links such as
bridges and railways behind enemy lines. Alerted by radio message
and by the BBC, French resistance men and women now leapt into
action with a large sabotage campaign.

Facing the ground troops was Hitler's Atlantic Wall, a series of
concrete bunkers looking out towards the sea. These were manned

by Germans with machine guns and mortars. The wall stretched from France's border with Spain, along the Bay of Biscay, the English Channel and the North Sea to the northernmost tip of Norway inside the Arctic Circle. Supplementing these fearsome bunkers were minefields and anti-landing-craft obstacles strewn over the beaches. Often the bunkers were located above the beaches on dunes, giving the Germans a bird's-eye view of the invading troops below. This was a big advantage for the defenders. The most strongly defended beach was Omaha and the struggles of the US troops to get off the beach are superbly reconstructed in the film *The Longest Day* while the horrors of the landings are brilliantly recreated in Steven Spielberg's movie *Saving Private Ryan*.

There were many gaps in the Atlantic Wall and some of the terrain was kinder. To the east of Omaha, troops had a simpler—but by no means easy—task on Gold Beach. The Durham troops were the second wave to land and they set foot on French soil at noon almost four years to the day after some of them had left as a defeated army from the beaches of Dunkirk. Accompanying all of the D-Day landings was the constant noise of thousands of aircraft overhead heading inland to bomb German targets. At sea there was a vast armada of ships, transport, supply and warships, supporting the invasion either by ferrying troops, equipment, fuel and other supplies or by shelling the Wehrmacht inland. On Gold Beach, the first wave had established the beachhead and the plan was for the Durhams to move quickly inland, link up with the first wave and secure the Caen–Bayeux road.

The Germans were caught by surprise. Some of their best troops and tanks sitting idly inland from the Pas de Calais waiting for the invasion that never happened thanks to *Plan Fortitude,* but those in Normandy didn't expect the allies to land in the bad weather. However, they quickly rallied and, for the next three months, fought

with great determination and skill, and not a little courage, in a
vain attempt to drive the invaders back into the sea.

The three Durham Battalions, who were part of the 50th
Armoured Division, were involved in only minor skirmishes at first.
Montgomery had hopes of capturing the important city Caen on 6
June, but the fighting qualities of the Wehrmacht meant that this
didn't happen until the beginning of August. Instead the Allies had
to fight for each field, barn, house, village, hedgerow and orchard
against a very determined enemy. The roads were narrow, making
it difficult for tanks to manoeuvre and the hedges surrounding the
fields tall and thick making it often impossible to know who was
on the other side. A ditch on either side of these bocage hedges
made it difficult for tanks to break through.

Slowly the Durhams made their way inland. There were a series
of fierce battles with the Wehrmacht, most notably at the village
of St. Pierre which the DLI first captured and then held despite a
ferocious counter-attack. Every planned advance was preceded by
a barrage from the air and perhaps the sea so that, when troops
finally reached their destinations, there was often hardly a building
left standing. Many of the few still intact were often booby trapped
by the Germans. Snipers were everywhere, concealed in buildings
and trees. Many an Allied soldier died from a single sniper's bullet.

The Germans held the advantage in many ways. They had to
defend a very narrow front unlike, for example, in Russia where
the fronts could stretch for hundreds of miles. Some of their
weapons were superior to those of the Allies. The Tiger tank was
better than anything the Allies had and their 88mm field guns
were both accurate and devastating. They used every trick in the
book. Everything was camouflaged: men, tanks and vehicles. The
Wehrmacht possessed a repertoire of dirty tricks, including leaving
booby traps in foxholes which had been evacuated and stringing wire

across roads to decapitate drivers of small vehicles. The Germans were, however, heavily outnumbered both in men and machines and the Allies had total command of the air.

The DLI and other veteran Allied troops were exhausted quite early in the campaign. But they persevered and triumphed in the very tough battle at Tilly-sur-Seulles. The 30th Army Corps had initially seized this strategically important village but, in a ten-day period from 8 June, possession changed hands more than twenty times. Finally, on 19 June, the Durhams and the rest of the 50th Division arrived to gain control once and for all and the Germans retreated.

The Germans were on the run but didn't give up easily and the DLI's next great battle came towards the end of July at Le Plessis Grimault. This was another very tough encounter and the enemy were only finally beaten after the 8th Battalion of the DLI, supported by tanks, engaged them in close-quarter fighting with grenades and automatic machine guns, taking over one hundred prisoners in the process.

By now many of them were suffering from dysentery and the three battalions were rested until 18 August. Meanwhile the Germans were being driven out of Normandy by other Allied forces. The campaign ended towards the end of August when one hundred thousand Germans were killed, wounded or captured in the "Falaise Pocket". The roads to the rest of France were now open.

During the campaign a quarter of a million Germans were killed or wounded. A further two hundred thousand were taken prisoner. Of the Allies, over two hundred thousand were killed or wounded and sixteen thousand aircrew died or went missing. As the Durhams made their way out of Normandy, scenes of utter devastation met them wherever they went. Roads were littered with dead soldiers, horses and abandoned vehicles. The fields were filled with the rotting carcases of dead cows and the stench was foul. Those cows still alive hadn't been milked in weeks and stood moaning in agony in the pastures. The pre-invasion bombing, coupled with further bombing during the campaign, killed over thirty thousand French civilians. Even after the soldiers left, people continued to die from unexploded bombs, mines and grenades.

Both sides committed war crimes. The SS carried out random massacres of civilians and prisoners as they retreated. French resistance fighters executed SS troops and members of the Gestapo without trial. The Allies occasionally hadn't time to deal with prisoners so they shot them instead. Like the French Resistance, they often shot captured SS personal without trial. It was the refusal of the SS soldiers (Waffen SS) to surrender that prolonged the campaign. These, the most fanatical of German soldiers, fought like demons as did the Hitler Youth battalions, many of whom were teenagers. All preferred death to surrender. German soldiers who deserted or lost heart were executed. Allied troops in the same boat were sent for mental rehabilitation.

Another big factor in the Allied victory was their superior leadership. Their Supreme Commander was an American, Dwight D Eisenhower (later US President) who somehow managed to control the big egos of the British and American Generals who were forever falling out with each other. The German supreme commander was Hitler himself whose only experience as a soldier was as a Corporal who was gassed in the trenches during the Great War. Hitler spent the final years of the Second World War studying maps, planning campaigns and issuing orders to generals without having the faintest idea of the local conditions such as weather, topography or position of enemy troops. The Wehrmacht had some very capable generals, but many of them were terrified of standing up to the Führer for fear of the sack or even worse. With Hitler in charge, it's a wonder that the war lasted as long as it did.

There are countless books about the Normandy campaign. One of the best is *D-Day: The Battle for Normandy* by Antony Beevor. It was the campaign which, in conjunction with *Operation Bagration* on the Eastern Front, finally guaranteed that Germany would lose the war in Europe. It was also the campaign which liberated France because, apart from small-scale skirmishes as the German Army retreated, there were no more major battles on French soil. The killing fields of Operation Overlord are a stark reminder of what the Allies owed to the people of Normandy.

The 5th and 7th Battalions of the DLI also played a major role in the closing months of the war. Both had spent most of their time in England as searchlight artillery battalions, doing their best to shoot the Luftwaffe out of the sky. The 7th landed in France towards the end of June and immediately became infantry and marched to Falaise. Artillery duties were resumed on 23 August and the River Seine was crossed. They raced for the Belgian border and then into the Netherlands before Nijmegen was reached in September.

The 5th had spent most of the war in Yorkshire. They were all territorials. Some members of the battalion, now part of the 113th Light Anti-Aircraft Regiment, landed on Juno Beach in Normandy in June and linked with XII Corps. Joining the chase of the Germans across France, they reached Brussels in September. The remaining soldiers of the 5th didn't reach France until November and they too headed for Brussels.

The American and Free French troops sped across country and reached Paris which they liberated without too much difficulty. The British forces, including five DLI battalions (the 10th and 11th had landed in Normandy shortly after D-Day) marched north towards the Pas de Calais where they were desperately keen to overrun and put out of action the German launch sites of the V1 and V2 rockets which were causing havoc as they fell on London and South East England. Small pockets of Germans provided sporadic resistance but generally this was not threatening. The Belgian frontier was crossed on 6 September 1944. Both in France and Belgium villagers and townsfolk greeted them with great flag-waving enthusiasm after four dark years of German occupation.

Any chance that the war would be over by Christmas disappeared soon after the Durhams left Brussels. The Germans were utterly determined to defend their own borders. As they retreated they blew up bridges and laid minefields. The Wehrmacht first set up a strong defensive line along the Albert Canal which linked Liege to Antwerp north of Brussels. A fierce battle ensued and the enemy were only thrown back after frantic close-quarter fighting. The Durhams and the rest of the Allied forces then crossed the Albert Canal at night. Replacing the bridges destroyed by the Germans was still causing some problems although the engineers worked hard and effectively. The Germans were having none of it and counter-attacked fiercely towards Geel. The Durhams suffered heavy casualties in defending against this attack but they held firm and the Germans fled northwards.

Montgomery tried to shorten the war by an airborne attack designed to seize the Rhine bridges. For once the Allies found themselves on the receiving end and, at Arnhem in the Netherlands, suffered a heavy defeat. They did, however, seize the bridge at Nijmegen (which looked a little bit like the Tyne Bridge in Newcastle) and the Durham Infantry and Artillery were charged with holding it, which they did. However hard the Germans fought, for them the war was lost. Two DLI battalions were sent home before Christmas, along with one of the artillery battalions. The two remaining battalions, the 9th Infantry and the 113th LA Regiment Artillery, then played a decisive role in the final victory.

Sint Joost was the scene of the final battle on Dutch soil and, on snow-covered ground, the Germans were defeated and driven back towards their own borders. The Durham Artillery men were briefly sent south to the Ardennes on Christmas Day 1944 where they helped in throwing back the last big German attack of the war at the "Battle of the Bulge". Back in the Netherlands, the next step was the crossing of the Rhine and the Durham Artillery pounded the Germans on the far side with the terrifying land mattress rockets which fired up to sixteen rockets in rapid succession, causing havoc amongst the defenders. Allied troops were soon over the river. The Durhams became the first British artillery unit to cross the Rhine.

The march through Germany began with bloody street fighting at Stadtlohn where more than three hundred Germans were killed. The troops paused briefly at Haldern after which the DLI Artillery split into two groups. One group joined the Infantry on the push into Hamburg, capturing hundreds of Germans *en route*, some as young as thirteen! Hamburg was reached on 1 May and, two days later, all German armies fighting in their homeland surrendered. Shortly afterwards the DLI led the way into Hamburg. All fighting in Europe ceased on 7 May and, on the following day, millions celebrated Victory in Europe (VE) Day. The Durham Light Infantry had been involved at the start of the war, in Northern France, and now, in their finest moment, they were there at the triumphant end. In July 1945, they reached Berlin.

This is not quite the end of their story. Back at Haldern in April, the remaining men of the 113th Light AA Regiment, which was now attached to the British VIIIth Corps and included many Durham soldiers, set off for a place of which they'd never heard—Belsen.

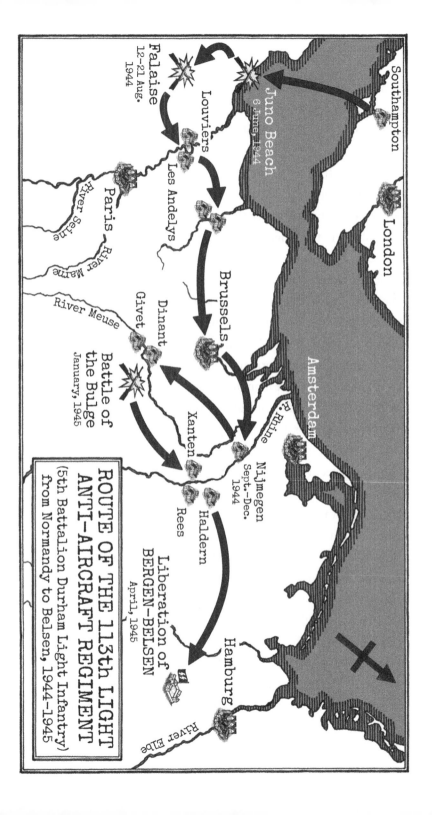

ROUTE OF THE 113th LIGHT
ANTI-AIRCRAFT REGIMENT
(5th Battalion Durham Light Infantry)
from Normandy to Belsen, 1944-1945

Southampton

London

Amsterdam

Paris

River Seine

River Marne

River Meuse

Falaise
12-21 Aug.
1944

Louviers

Les Andelys

Juno Beach
6 June, 1944

Brussels

Givet

Dinant

Battle of
the Bulge
January, 1945

Xanten

Rees

Haldern

R. Rhine

Nijmegen
Sept.-Dec.
1944

Liberation of
BERGEN-BELSEN
April, 1945

Hamburg

River Elbe

CHAPTER SIX

LIBERATION
Belsen April–May 1945

I hear and I forget. I see and I
remember. I do and I understand.
Confucius

The Allies' Second Army were making great inroads into the heart
of Northern Germany in April 1945. German defeat was inevitable.
It was only a matter of time before the crumbling structure of the
Third Reich collapsed into rubble. Yet the Germans fought on,
especially in the east where the huge Red Army was battling its
way towards Berlin. Before victory was finally won, one hundred
thousand Soviet soldiers would die in the Battle for Berlin.

The situation was different in the west. True, there were still
pockets of resistance, but even Hitler, in his bunker beneath the
Reich Chancellery in the capital, recognised the inevitably of
defeat. However, he still hoped that some kind of agreement could
be reached with the Allies. In the madness of his final days, the
Führer actually believed that the Allies might join with Germany in
defeating what he believed was their real enemy, the Soviet Union.
Only Himmler made any attempt to broker any kind of peace, but
the Allies had already decided that unconditional surrender would

be the only outcome of the war in Europe. The German people in the east had already had a taste of Russian barbarity when the Soviet troops had carried out tens of thousands of rapes, random killings of civilians, looting and wanton destruction of property. As the Red Army advanced on Berlin through Eastern Germany, countless Germans headed west in the hope of receiving better treatment from the Allies.

In Belsen the situation was desperate and getting worse every day. Thousands of prisoners were in urgent need of medical attention and food, without which they would die. The death toll amongst the inmates mounted every hour. Most of those who remained were waiting for death. A number of recent arrivals not suffering from typhus were in reasonable health, although TB and dysentery began to take hold. Many SS guards had already fled and the watchtowers were deserted from 11 April. Most of the men who remained began to treat the prisoners less harshly in the hope that this might count in their favour when Germany's defeat became final. The SS women, however, continued to behave in a barbaric manner. Even as the Allied soldiers began to arrive, the SS shot a small number of prisoners who were trying to steal from the food store. The Wehrmacht were terrified that if those prisoners with just a tiny amount of strength left broke out, disease would spread like wildfire to the surrounding countryside. On top of the disease, starvation was beginning to be the biggest problem of all. On the final days before the relief of the camp, the inmates had been without even the smallest amount of food and water for four days. Himmler, going back on his previous order that all the prisoners should be killed, agreed that the camp should be handed over to the Allies and a ceasefire arranged. Allied and Wehrmacht officers met on 12 April and a truce was signed in the early hours of the following day. An area of nineteen square miles around Belsen was

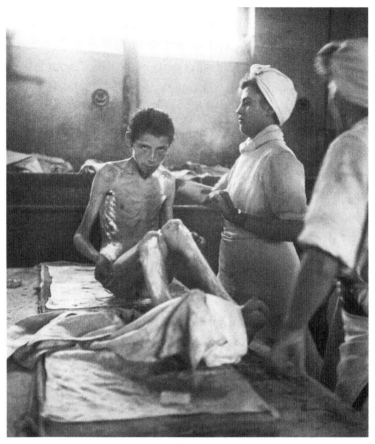

**Figure 10: An emaciated young boy is dusted with
DDT powder to protect him against typhus by a
German nurse (photo: © IWM, BU 5473).**

declared a neutral zone. Those SS personnel still at the camp were
told to remain and help to keep order. They would be assisted by
eight hundred German and fifteen hundred Hungarian soldiers
who would be responsible for guarding the camp perimeter fencing.
The Hungarians were armed and wore a white arm band on the
left sleeve. In accordance with the terms of the truce, the Germans
soon left but the Hungarians stayed until 5 May when they were

relieved by a unit of Soviet prisoners of war from the POW camp that was adjacent to the Wehrmacht barracks.

On 15 April 1945, the advance party of the Allied Army arrived at Belsen, accompanied by the camp's commandant, Josef Kramer. The Allied troops were from the 11th Armoured Division. Lance Bombardier of the Oxford Yeomanry was one of the first into the camp and recently he told his story to the *Daily Mail* (2 April 2011). The Germans were told to erect warning signs saying *TYPHUS!* around the outside of the camp. Nobody was allowed to leave but loudspeakers told the prisoners that the British had arrived. They were free and food and medical attention were on their way. They were hardly free: free perhaps from bullying, harassment and murder by the SS but most were very seriously ill. It was obvious to the British that quick action was essential to save lives and prevent the disease from spreading further. SS personnel, mainly cooks and clerks, but with a small number of guards, were put to work alongside the German and Hungarian soldiers. As part of the truce, the Allies agreed to release Wehrmacht soldiers after six days. These would then return with their weapons to the front line. The German army officers made it clear that they didn't care what happened to the SS members. They hated them almost as much as the prisoners did. This seems to have given the British soldiers the go-ahead to exact some kind of revenge on the SS for their murderous behaviour throughout the war. The Nazis were kicked, punched, stabbed with bayonets, worked to death disposing of the corpses or shot in the very early days after the liberation of the camp.

The immense problems at Belsen wouldn't be solved without considerable re-enforcements, including medical staff, food, water and medicines. In any case, the 11th Armoured Division, complete with tanks, was needed elsewhere to do battle with the final remaining pockets of German resistance. As they left, a far

Figure 11: Inside the cleansing station, women and children prepare to bathe (photo: © IWM, BU 5460).

larger party of soldiers arrived on 18 April. These included troops of the 113th Light Anti-Aircraft Battalion of the Royal Artillery of which the 5th Battalion Durham Light Infantry was now a significant part. They had covered two hundred and thirty-eight miles in twenty-two hours to reach Belsen. As they approached Belsen they were struck by how peaceful everything seemed. The war obviously hadn't reached that part of Germany. Cows grazed in the lush green fields and the rural community went about their business as if nothing would disturb their lives. On arrival at Belsen the circumstances couldn't have provided a greater contrast. What these young soldiers found when they reached the camp was almost beyond belief. There were great mounds of bodies everywhere. Some of them had obviously been there for some time and were rotting. The trenches which had been dug as latrines were crammed full of corpses.

> The inmates had lost all self-respect and degraded morally to the level of beasts. Their clothes were in rags and teeming with lice; they had no eating utensils or plates and at the time of the food distribution behaved more like ravenous wolves than human beings.
>
> *From* The Story of Belsen *by Captain Andrew Pares, adjutant of the 113th Light Anti-Aircraft Regiment of the Royal Artillery (Durham County Record Office D/DLI 7/404/10)*

The huts were absolutely appalling. They'd been built to accommodate one hundred people but in some more than five hundred people were packed like sardines. The dead, the dying and the desperately ill were crammed into the bunks or littered the floor. All of them were either naked or dressed in flimsy rags. Lice crawled over all of these skeletal creatures. As the soldiers gasped in horror at this scene from hell, one or two prisoners gave up the fight and died. Today we talk of post-traumatic stress in war but it is difficult to believe that a modern soldier has experienced anything approaching the revulsion and shock that these Durhams must have felt on that early spring day in 1945. What they saw on that day remained with them for the rest of their lives. Paul Armstrong, a DLI officer from Bishop Auckland remembers:

> I saw the ovens. I saw where they hanged them. I saw the place where they gathered false teeth and where they stored the hair. I can't describe further what it was like, but the horrifying [thing] was that a village nearby, where the

trains carrying these people had to pass through to get to the camp, these people pretended that they had no idea. The officer that took over forced them at gunpoint—all the villagers—to go and walk round the camp to see what the German soldiers had done, because they were pretending that they knew nothing about it. He made sure that they did.

**Paul Armstrong (IWM Sound
Archives, recording no. 14974)**

About fifty thousand were still alive at the time of the liberation. The Allies now had to speedily perform a number of very urgent tasks before more were lost. Food and water were desperately needed. Prisoners had to be deloused, the most seriously ill transferred to hospital and the dead buried. The Allied officers were so appalled by what they saw that they immediately ordered the arrest of Kramer and the remaining SS guards which included Irma Grese. Some of the fitter male prisoners looted the SS food stores which were luxuriously provisioned. Others set off for the nearby barracks where the hated kapos, those criminal prisoners acting as auxiliary guards, were living. These men and women had been almost as bad as, if not worse than, the SS guards and had conducted their own reign of terror. The prisoners forced the kapos to the top floor and threw them out of the windows. One hundred and fifty died in this manner. The Allied soldiers turned a blind eye.

Of the fifty thousand survivors, about half were women and more than two-thirds of these were Jewish, most of whom had been transferred from the evacuated death camps of Eastern Europe. Virtually all of them had lost many, if not all, of their family members in the gas chambers of Auschwitz, Sobibor, Treblinka, Chelmno, Belzec and elsewhere. They represented, as one British soldier remarked, most of what was left of the European Jews.

The Allies were now in a race against time to save as many lives as possible. Water tankers with cooking equipment and food had already arrived by the time that the Durham soldiers reached the camp. Most of the food was canned and inmates devoured the contents at great speed. It was a serious mistake. They'd gone without proper food for so long that their stomachs had shrunk and they were totally unable to digest the kind of food that soldiers had lived on throughout the war. They were immediately ill with vomiting and diarrhoea. Two thousand of them died. Private Richard Atkinson was from Jarrow:

> We started giving them tins of bully beef and we killed them.
>
> ### Richard Atkinson (IWM Sound
> ### Archives, recording no. 14792)

The Allied soldiers were utterly shaken with shock and disgust when they saw the full extent of the horror in the camp. There was even evidence of cannibalism amongst the prisoners as bodies lay around without flesh and with missing kidneys, livers and hearts. Such was the depth of inhumanity to which some had sunk following their atrocious treatment. Some internees were found to have been subjected to medical experiments or compulsory sterilisation. A few took their revenge and SS staff covered in blood became a regular sight. Wehrmacht troops, who had had no direct role in the terror in Belsen, were pushed about and bullied by Allied troops. The overpowering stench of death and excrement was too much for many and they too became, for a brief period, violently sick. Major Allan of the 113th Light Anti-Aircraft Battalion remembers the fear of infection:

> I was frightened to death [of catching typhus]. We were
> all frightened because typhus was rampant. We thought
> we might get the disease transmitted. It never happened.
> People got ill through psychological conditions and so on.
> The men were well powdered before and after leaving the
> diseased area.
>
> *Alexander Smith Allan (IWM Sound*
> *Archives, recording no. 11903)*

Professional help was at hand with the arrival of Brigadier Glyn Hughes, Chief Medical Officer of the Second Army. Hughes quickly took stock of the situation. By his reckoning, about three-quarters of the camp population needed medical attention. Many of these, up to ten thousand, would quickly die without help. Medical staff, medicines and hospital beds were urgently needed. A two-hundred-strong field ambulance unit arrived. This was nowhere near enough to cope with the rapidly deteriorating situation. The unit was bolstered by a small number of trained nurses and doctors from those liberated prisoners who were still in reasonable health. They did a fantastic job. The soldiers threw wounded soldiers out of the nearby military hospital and told the medical staff there to help care for the Belsen inmates. This they did, reluctantly at first, but soon with great commitment as they saw the state of the sick and dying. Germans manned an area set aside for decontamination where survivors were bathed, the men shaved and all sprayed with DDT delousing powder. They were joined by medical staff from the nearby German town of Celle. The barracks at the Wehrmacht tank training school, about half a mile to the north, was converted into another hospital.

On 19 April 1945, the world first learned about the Belsen concentration camp. BBC reporter Richard Dimbleby (father of

David and Jonathan) arrived at Belsen with the first wave of soldiers on 15 April. Television programmes weren't broadcast during the war so Dimbleby's broadcast would be on the Home Service of BBC radio. He recorded a report in which all of the gruesome detail of the camp was fully and graphically described. The world was stunned.

Listeners learned that over the previous few months thirty thousand prisoners had died, mostly due to neglect, and that more than twenty-five thousand were still either desperately ill or dying from starvation or disease. Some prisoners—recent arrivals, he assumed—were in reasonable health (a number of these must have been responsible for throwing the kapos out of the high windows), but inside the wire he saw thousands shuffling about in a cloud of dust, accompanied by the pungent smell of death.

Dimbleby spent some time inside the huts and was utterly appalled by what he saw:

> Inside the huts it was even worse. I've seen many terrible sights in the last five years but nothing, nothing approaching the dreadful interior of this hut at Belsen. The dead and the dying lay close together. I picked my way over corpse after corpse in the gloom until I heard one voice that rose above the gentle undulating moaning. I found a girl. She was a living skeleton, impossible to gauge her age for she had practically no hair left on her head and her face was only a yellow parchment sheet with two holes in it for eyes. She was stretching out her stick of an arm and gasping something, it was "English, English, medicine, medicine." And she was trying to cry but had not enough strength.
>
> **Richard Dimbleby, BBC Home Service, April 1945**
> **(IWM Sound Archives, recording no. 17714)**

Throughout the liberation, the Army Film Unit was shooting footage detailing the horrors of Belsen in full. The importance of the media and the part it played in the liberation of Belsen in influencing world opinion and post-war attitudes will be discussed in the next chapter.

Instead of firing powerful artillery weapons at the retreating Wehrmacht over the Rhine, the Durhams found themselves collecting the dead and living from the overcrowded huts. Their burial roles were supervisory because the Germans, including the SS, lifted the corpses from the piles and took them to lorries from where they were transported to mass graves. As each grave filled up, new ones were dug by the Germans and Hungarians. Each grave contained up to five hundred corpses. Up to seventeen hundred were buried in one day and seventeen thousand were interred in total. Such was the volume of corpses that had to be dealt with, bulldozers were brought in to speed up the process. While the Germans performed this gruesome task, survivors and Allied soldiers stood by and hurled insults at them. Any Nazi who attempted to run away was shot. Several were but, after the arrival of the Durhams with the 113th Light Anti-Aircraft Battalion, there was no evidence of unnecessary brutality:

> Yes I remember the CO [Commanding Officer] Colonel Mather. He told everybody we must be careful to contain our feelings and not allow ourselves to become brutalised as the Germans had, and not be unduly out of control.
>
> **_Alexander Smith Allan (IWM Sound_**
> **_Archives, recording no. 11903)_**

The Durham soldiers did:

> I have the greatest admiration for the Geordies and I think
> the people from the North East were hard but extremely fair.
>
> *Alexander Smith Allan (IWM Sound*
> *Archives, recording no. 11903)*

To the Durhams and other Allied troops fell the unenviable task of clearing the huts. Working in pairs, they carried the dead and gravely ill on stretchers, either to be buried by the Germans or for onward transportation to hospital. All day they worked in these terrible conditions with the smell of death all around them.

Hughes and his team did a fantastic job and introduced the "Bengal Famine Diet" which slowly began to alleviate the starvation problem. But still they were fighting against great odds. Seven thousand died in the first week and deaths over the first ten days after liberation averaged five hundred a day and this included twenty SS personnel who contracted typhus. The clearing of the huts was extremely difficult. The soldiers had to distinguish between the living and the dead and this was not easy because many of those still alive were barely so. Four hundred a day were carefully moved. Those still alive were first given the clean up by the Germans at the delousing area and then taken to hospital.

After the initial high mortality rate, the numbers dying gradually decreased. The outstanding work of Brigadier Hughes and his team, supported by the German and ex-prisoner medical staff meant that more than two-thirds of the original fifty thousand alive at the time of the liberation survived. One by one the huts were cleared until, on 19 May 1945, they were deserted. Two days later they were destroyed by fire. The notorious Bergen-Belsen concentration camp no longer existed. It was gone but by no means forgotten, not least by the troops of the Durham Light Infantry.

There have been many books written about Belsen and its liberation. *After Daybreak* by Ben Shepherd is a superbly researched and brilliantly written account of the events of April and early May, 1945. Amongst the numerous memoirs of the prisoners *The Diary of Bergen-Belsen 1944–45* by Hanna Lévy-Hass and *I was a Boy in Belsen* by Tomi Reichental are moving and harrowing books about life in the notorious camp.

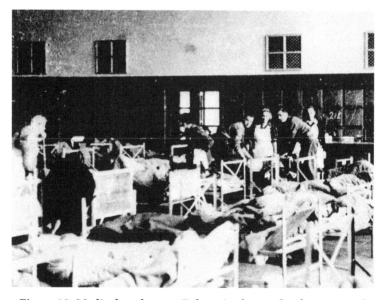

Figure 12: Medical students at Belsen, in the wards of a converted
building "round house hospital", looking after patients in
1945 (photo: The RAMC Muniment Collection in the care of
the Wellcome Library; Wellcome Images, no. L0029088).

CHAPTER SEVEN

AFTERWARDS

Who has inflicted this upon us? Who has made
us Jews different from all other people?
Anne Frank, *Diary of a Young Girl* (published 1947)

The Survivors

Nobody seems quite sure about the exact figure of those who survived or died at Belsen. On arrival on 15 April 1945, the British soldiers found between forty and fifty thousand survivors as well as over ten thousand corpses. More than thirty thousand had already died. Because of the meticulous record keeping of the British medical teams, we know that the numbers of those who died between the camp's liberation on 15 April and its destruction a little over a month later was around fourteen thousand. Many had died of typhus and many more of starvation. There were between twenty-five and thirty thousand survivors. Given the excellent medical care that these unfortunate people received, few will have died either of typhus or starvation after May 1945. However, a new killer was on the loose: tuberculosis (TB), for which an effective medical treatment only became available a year or so later. Many survivors may have succumbed to this disease, possibly up to five years later.

It's only an estimate but perhaps as many as twenty thousand did survive. What happened to them? Before tracing just a handful, it's important to understand the situation in Europe in the summer of 1945. Everywhere people were on the move. Germans who had settled in conquered lands were thrown out of Poland, Czechoslovakia, the Soviet Union and elsewhere. Even parts of pre-war Germany fell into foreign hands. East Prussia became part of the Soviet Union and parts of North East Germany were given to Poland. The Russians expelled Poles from the Ukraine and the Poles sent Ukrainians back to the Soviet Union. Parts of Eastern Poland were seized by the USSR. It was a total shambles and all over Europe, people were on the roads trying to find somewhere to live. Displaced Persons' (DP) camps sprung up everywhere. One of these was at Belsen, next to the recently destroyed concentration camp. Many survivors lived there, some for years. Astonishingly, some returned home to Poland, Czechoslovakia, Hungary, the Netherlands and other countries to find they were not welcome. Eastern Europe was in the grip of Soviet domination. Many Jews felt that this was little better than the Nazi regime that had preceded it. Of the three million Polish Jews that were alive in September 1939, less than half a million had survived by May 1945. Most had been murdered in the extermination camps. Even after the war there were outbreaks of anti-Jewish violence (pogroms) in Poland, most notably at Kielce where forty two died. In one of the finest of all documentary films about the Second World War, *Night Will Fall*, a Polish woman survivor of Belsen tells the audience that she did not wish to return to the country of her birth. Whether this was because of the Soviet presence or through fear of anti-Semitic violence isn't clear. That's not to say that all Poles hated the Jews. The vast majority didn't but there were enough who did and this, combined with the threat of Russian cruelty, persuaded many of the Jewish Belsen survivors from Poland not to return home.

Figure 13: Wooden cross erected in 1945 by Polish
survivors, 2010. Bergen-Belsen Memorial (photo:
Lower Saxony Memorials Foundation).

Many stayed in the DP camp while others tried to emigrate to the USA, Britain, Canada and other states but even there they were not always welcome. For many, however, their dream was to live in Palestine, their "promised land". At first this was not easy to achieve. The British were in charge and were anxious not to let in too many Jews for fear of offending the Arab population. Eventually, in 1948, the state of Israel was established and tens of thousands of Jews were able to settle there and build a new nation.

Exactly what happened to the majority of survivors is not known. Even Ben Shepherd, in his superb and painstakingly researched book *After Daybreak,* was unable to trace a significant number. Countless returned to their countries of origin to seek news of relatives. All over Europe in the summer of 1945 there were lists of those who had died, those who had survived and those whose whereabouts were unknown.

Many accounts have been written by survivors of life in Belsen. Chapters Four and Five told two of these stories. Hanna Lévy-Hass, the author of *Diary of Bergen-Belsen 1944–1945,* was thirty-two in 1945. She'd been born in Sarajevo, then part of Yugoslavia, but now the capital of Bosnia-Herzegovina. During the war she'd fought as a partisan against the German occupiers. Arrested by the Gestapo in June 1944, she was at first imprisoned in her own country and later sent to Belsen. Before the liberation she was packed on to a train bound for Czechoslovakia by the SS. She escaped during the journey and was rescued by the advancing Red Army. She was in Belgrade later that summer and here she learned that ten of her relatives had been murdered by the Nazis, including her mother and sister who were gassed in the back of a sealed truck. Hanna emigrated to Israel in 1948. Later she briefly returned to the former Yugoslavia but died in Jerusalem in 2001, carrying with her to the grave the emotional scars of her time in Belsen which had troubled her for more than fifty years.

Tomi Reichental was Slovakian and was just nine when he was sent to Belsen. He returned to his home village after leaving Belsen to be reunited with those members of his family who had survived the Holocaust. Here he found that twenty-four other members of his family: grandparents, cousins, uncles and aunts, had died in the death camps. Twenty of these had been gassed in Auschwitz, three killed in Buchenwald and one had died at Belsen.

Tomi and other members of his family left Europe for Israel in 1949. Here he later qualified as an engineer and went to the Republic of Ireland to work in 1959. In 1961 he met, and later married, an Irish girl. They had three sons. Tomi was reluctant to talk of his time in Belsen but in later life he contributed a great deal to Holocaust education and talked to groups in schools, colleges, universities and elsewhere as well as playing a major part in the documentary film *Till the Tenth Generation* (2008). His in many ways uplifting story is told in *I was a Boy in Belsen*.

The Germans

The signing of the truce between the advancing Allies and the retreating Germans on 15 April included a clause in which it was agreed that Wehrmacht troops should be released as soon as the British took control of the camp. The SS were excluded from this agreement. The Wehrmacht left it up to the Allies to do as they wished with the SS. Most of these were put to work moving corpses and preparing and filling mass graves. Predominantly these were domestic staff, including cooks and clerks, but there were some guards. Seventy-seven SS guards and their superiors were arrested on 16 April. It was the intention of the British Army to prosecute these men and women for war crimes.

Between arrest and trial, some SS staff fell ill and by the time of the legal proceedings were either dead or too ill to appear. Three SS men were shot trying to escape and one committed suicide. This left forty-five men and women to be tried by a British military tribunal and charged with war crimes. In the aftermath of the Second World War there were numerous war crimes trials both in Europe and

Figure 14: Irma Grese standing in the courtyard of the prisoner-of-war cage at Celle with Josef Kramer. Both were convicted of war crimes and sentenced to death (photo: © IWM, BU 9745).

Japan. The best known were held in Nuremberg between 1945 and 1946. Here the leading Nazis were tried, convicted or acquitted and those found guilty were hanged or imprisoned.

Belsen was one of the very first of these trials and opened in the North German town of Luneburg on 17 September 1945. By this time the number of defendants had been reduced to forty-four, serious illness had removed another from the final legal proceedings. Charges of war crimes and war crimes against citizens of Allied countries were read to them. All pleaded not guilty. SS men and women who had previously been at Auschwitz were also charged with the crimes committed there. This included the camp commandant Josef Kramer, camp doctor Fritz Klein, Elizabeth Volkenrath, senior woman guard, and Irma Grese.

Massive public interest was generated by the trial and there were more than one hundred media representatives in attendance. The defendants were accused of ill-treating and killing named persons and others. Not all fifty thousand victims could appear on the charge sheet. Amongst the witnesses for the prosecution were British soldiers, who reported what they found on arrival at Belsen, and survivors. Testimonies from survivors too ill to attend were read out to the court. The trial lasted fifty-four days. One day was set aside for viewing film of the camp on liberation made by the Army Film Unit and another for a visit to the camp itself.

The Nazis' defence was conducted by British Army lawyers. Kramer defended himself by claiming that he was only following orders, that he had tried, without success, to have food sent to the camp, that he had been forced by a higher authority to accept tens of thousands of prisoners with which the camp could not cope, that Allied air attacks had disrupted the delivery of supplies and that bombing from them had put the pumps that supplied water out of action. The 15 April truce, he argued, gave him immunity from prosecution. He denied killing any prisoner intentionally.

Whether or not these arguments, and some similar ones from his co-defendants, had any effect on the verdicts will never be known but Kramer's records at Auschwitz certainly condemned him. His responsibility there had been to select prisoners on arrival to work or to die. Fritz Klein had carried out sadistic medical experiments at Auschwitz and Volkenrath and Grese had certainly murdered prisoners there.

These four were amongst those found guilty and sentenced to death on 17 November 1945. Seven others were also sent to the gallows. Three of these had also been at Auschwitz. Of the remainder, nineteen were sentenced to terms of imprisonment of between one and fifteen years. Some had their sentences reduced on appeal and the last of the Belsen convicts was released in 1955.

Kramer and the ten others were hanged in Hamelin prison on 17 December 1945. The gruesome duties were carried out by Albert Pierrepoint, Britain's most experienced hangman. In a career lasting over a quarter of a century, Pierrepoint executed four hundred and thirty-five persons. Over two hundred of these were war criminals in post-war Germany.

Almost a year later there was a further execution when a brutal former Belsen kapo (a prisoner given temporary supervisory responsibility) was arrested in the Netherlands and charged with beating prisoners at Belsen to death. He was hanged on 11 October 1946.

Journalists in France and the Soviet Union thought that some of the sentences were too lenient. So did some of the survivors. But the trials had established a precedent, which operates even to this day, that war criminals should be held to account for their crimes. The Allies had agreed to vigorously prosecute war criminals as early as 1943. Belsen was one of the first places that this happened. The Belsen trial was an example of one of the earliest occasions during which film was used as evidence. Film of the trial was made and parts of it can be seen in *Night Will Fall* and on *Pathé, British Movietone* and other newsreels of the time. The Imperial War Museum has superbly restored much of this footage and this will be shown publicly in April 2015 to coincide with the seventieth anniversary of the liberation of many of the camps. Entitled *German Concentration Camps: Factual Survey*, it was screened to great acclaim at film festivals around Europe. The trials, and the film, enabled the world to become aware of the treatment of prisoners at the most beastly of all of the horror camps, Auschwitz, for the first time.

The Camp

Today thousands each year visit the remaining concentration camps. Amongst these are Dachau (Southern Germany), Auschwitz and Sachsenhausen (near Berlin). Many go to these places to see where members of their families have died. Others visit to remind themselves of the horrors of the Holocaust, determined that it should never happen again. The camp at Belsen no longer exists. It was destroyed by the British in May 1945. Like so many wartime German sites, Belsen was huge, embracing a concentration camp, prisoner-of-war camp, forced labour camp, a military barracks and a hospital. Apart from the concentration and labour camps, these places continued to function after the huts were burned. The hospital, of course, as well as the military barracks, continued to

treat many of those still desperately ill after the liberation. Part of
the area became the largest displaced persons' camp in Germany,
looking after people who had nowhere to go. It wasn't until 1950,
when things had gradually returned to normal, that the DP camp
closed. Today the area is still used for training by NATO armed
forces.

Before Belsen was wiped from the immediate memory, important
local German citizens were forced to spend a period of time looking
at the results of the Nazi party's inhuman behaviour. Wherever a
camp was liberated in Western Germany and parts of Austria, this
same pattern was repeated. In the village of Burgsteinfurt (north-
west of Münster) citizens were marched at gunpoint to the local
cinema and forced to watch film of the liberation of the camps,
Atrocities: The Evidence. A total of four thousand attended the
various screenings.

Although Belsen has been a site of international remembrance
since 1945, it was more than twenty years before anything substantial
appeared there.

In the immediate aftermath of the war, the massive task of
rebuilding a shattered Europe appeared to take preference over
punishing many of those responsible for what became known as
the Holocaust. The Cold War between the Western Allies and the
Soviet Union and their reluctant East European allies led to a fear
of the future rather than remembrance of the past. Many people
chose to forget, but not the Jews, who began to hunt down those
responsible for the six million murders. Their big breakthrough
came in 1960 when Adolf Eichmann, one of the major organisers
of the "final solution to the Jewish problem", was kidnapped from
his refuge in Argentina by Israeli agents. Smuggled back to Israel,
Eichmann was interrogated for nine months before being tried and
convicted in Jerusalem in 1961. He was hanged in 1962.

The capture and trial of Eichmann seized the world's imagination and soon people did begin to remember the Holocaust. At Belsen an exhibition hall and document centre was opened. Over the years this has been greatly expanded. In 2005 a number of monuments for the dead were built. In 2007 a new Exhibition and Document Centre was built and this now receives up to three hundred thousand visitors each year. The Bergen-Belsen Memorial is fittingly located on Anne-Frank-Platz.

Figure 15: Signpost on Anne-Frank-Platz, 2011 (photo: Michael Pechel, Lower Saxony Memorials Foundation).

**Figure 16: Bergen-Belsen Memorial, 2010. Memorial
stones, Jewish monument, obelisk and inscription wall
(photo: Lower Saxony Memorials Foundation).**

The Soldiers and the Medical Staff

Not a vast amount of material exists about the soldiers' reaction to
the time that they spent at Belsen. When the bulk of the troops left
the camp in May 1945, the war was over. The Durhams and others
in the 113th Light AA Regiment were given a period of extended
leave after their terrible experiences and lazed on the silver sand
at Travemünde on the Baltic Coast. For many of them the next
stage was passage back to England, demobilisation and a return
to civilian life. For others the end of conflict saw them become
part of the army of occupation in Germany. The defeated enemy
was divided into four sectors with the Soviet Union in the north
and east, the Americans in the south and east, the French in the
south-west and the British in the north-west.

Virtually all cities in Germany, and many large towns as well,
were bombsites and, after much soul-searching, the Western Allies

decided that Germany must be rebuilt. So the DLI troops and others found themselves helping with the reconstruction of a country that had just, a short while before, been their enemy. Additionally, they had policing duties over the defeated nation and did assist with the tracking down and arrest of former Nazi party members. At the war's end they were in Hamburg and later in Berlin. Most, no doubt, remembered their time spent at Belsen. Paul Armstrong, whom we met in Chapter Six, later said:

> No, I would never forgive the Germans, never.
> ***IWM Sound Archives, recording no. 14974***

Private Richard Atkinson from Jarrow did his job and tried to put the horrors of Belsen behind him but later found this impossible:

> Knocked you out for a day or two . . . Left your mind until this film came out and you had to take them round again.
> ***IWM Sound Archives, recording no. 14972***

Many years later he admitted that he never wanted to be reminded of his experiences again:

> Now when it comes on television I don't want to watch it. I don't look. I don't want to see it. But you can still smell it.
> ***IWM Sound Archives, recording no. 14972***

Major Allan was left with a life-long hatred of Germany, and never wished to visit Germany after the war:

> I have no wish to associate myself with anything Germanic
> or German at all ... I have never been able to go into
> Germany. I once went to Cologne and I had to turn back.
>
> **IWM Sound Archives, recording no. 11903**

Major Walford remembered listening to a sergeant major soon
after the end of the war:

> He said to me that when he got a sight of Belsen "I will never
> forget that sight." He came from Hartlepool. "I will tell my
> children what went on in Germany, and particularly at Belsen.
>
> **IWM Sound Archives, recording no. 21797**

Time, it would seem, was not a great healer for the witnesses of
Belsen. We can safely assume that many soldiers were affected in
this way and were extremely reluctant to recount their experiences
when they reached home. Mervyn Payne, an officer who was one of
the first into the camp, many years later broke down when speaking
about his Belsen experience to members of a South Wales church
congregation. Unable to continue, he curtailed his address after
just five minutes.

 We know little or nothing about the medical staff. The student
volunteers returned to their studies in London, no doubt deeply
affected by their experiences, yet probably learning lessons that
would help to carry them through their medical careers. Brigadier
Glyn Hughes, in many ways the greatest hero of Belsen, became a
distinguished medical administrator. He helped in the creation of
the National Health Service (1948). Amongst many decorations he
received were the DSO for his army service and the CBE for what
he achieved in civilian life. In later life he was Honorary Physician
to the Queen. From 1955 to his death in 1973 he was the secretary

of the famous Barbarians Rugby Club. In 1959 he appeared on the television programme *This is Your Life,* but he will always be remembered as the man who saved so many lives at Belsen.

Of the nurses, some continued to serve in the Royal Army Medical Corps while others perhaps returned to Britain to work in the fledgling National Health Service. Many were left traumatised by their experiences for many years. An elderly lady, who died just a few years ago in Newcastle-upon-Tyne, left her native land, having served as a German nurse at Belsen. She, like so many others, spoke little of those terrible events. The Holocaust, in which six million Jewish men, women and children died, was one of the greatest crimes in human history. Most of those who committed those atrocities are now dead, either though execution, by their own hand or of natural causes. The few remaining war criminals are still being hunted down, tried, prosecuted and punished by the German government. Belsen played only a small part in the annals of horror but it is entirely understandable that those who witnessed the liberation and its aftermath were troubled by their experiences for the rest of their lives and found it so hard to forgive.

The Public Reaction

Belsen was not the first camp to be liberated. The Red Army had set free prisoners at Majdanek in Poland in July 1944 and overrun the almost-deserted Auschwitz six months later. The Russians, however, chose not to let the world know about these camps at the time. In the West, the Americans reached Buchenwald, near Weimar, in East Central Germany four days before the British reached Belsen. Following the US troops in was the legendary American broadcaster Edward R Murrow whose description of what he saw was heard by the American people just as the British were reaching Belsen.

The British public first heard of Belsen from Richard Dimbleby (see Chapter Six) and it was his report that established in the minds of people here at home the full extent of Nazi barbarity:

> I have never seen British soldiers so moved to cold fury as the men who opened the Belsen camp this week.
>
> **Richard Dimbleby, BBC Home Service, April 1945**
> **(IWM Sound Archives, recording no. 17714)**

Dimbleby then added his own assessment of the terrible effects of these camps on both inmate and guard:

> I realised that what is so ghastly is not so much the individual acts of barbarism that take place in SS camps but the gradual breakdown of civilisation that happens when human beings are herded like animals behind barbed wire.
>
> **Richard Dimbleby, BBC Home Service, April 1945**
> **(IWM Sound Archives, recording no. 17714)**

Dimbleby recorded his report before the arrival of the Durhams but we do know that their reaction was similar to his. It is easy to imagine how people back home received this news. In the 1940s BBC radio was the sole source of instant news. Television had been suspended for the duration of the war and there was no internet, of course. So when the nation tuned in to hear Dimbleby's broadcast on 19 April 1945, they were utterly devastated by what they heard.

Richard Dimbleby's BBC report from Belsen was a landmark in the history of broadcasting.

That the Jews had been persecuted by the Nazis was common knowledge. The disgraceful events of Kristallnacht in 1938 were widely reported and, during the war, several newspapers, including the *Daily Mail* and *The Daily Telegraph* in June 1942, had drawn attention to the killing of Jews in the camps but they didn't know the extent of it and nobody could have known of the inhuman treatment of the prisoners as was now evident at Belsen.

The newspapers covered the liberation but, at first, published few photographs. The *Daily Express* informed its readers that they could view the full horrors of Belsen as exhibitions of some of the photographs were to be displayed in their reading rooms throughout the country:

> PICTURES EVERY BRITISH CITIZEN SHOULD SEE
>
> Pictures of German atrocities which cannot be published in the newspapers are being placed on exhibition in Daily Express reading rooms throughout the country.
>
> Parents are advised that young children should not be taken to see these pictures. But a duty is imposed on citizens everywhere to investigate and to see for themselves the overwhelming mass of evidence that has been accumulated with the advance of the Allied armies.
>
> A special exhibition of enlarged pictures is being prepared. This will be on view at the Daily Express Reading Room at 299, Regent Street, London, at a date to be announced shortly.
>
> **Daily Express,** *21 April 1945*

The cinema newsreels were different. Millions visited the cinema each week and the weekly newsreel was always part of the programme.

However, the film studios (who often produced the newsreels) and the cinema owners were anxious not to alienate audiences by showing too much gruesome footage. The cinemas were, after all, places of entertainment where people came to escape the miseries of wartime life. Between 1939 and 1945 the newsreels did, of course, cover the war but images were often, but not always, accompanied by stirring music and the optimistic voice of the commentator. Restrictions on children seeing unsuitable material were in place then as today. The appalling scenes from Belsen were not suitable viewing for the young and it was certainly not the film industry's policy to restrict newsreel viewing to adults. However, such was the enormity of this story that the newsreels soon began to show the images from Belsen, although both *Pathé* and *British Movietone* did not use all of the footage at their disposal which included film of SS guards giving name, rank and so on in front of a pile of bodies. Other film of North East soldiers telling the SS guards to *get on with it* was not shown but, in a clip titled *In the Wake of the Hun* shown in cinemas from 22 April 1945, *Movietone* gave this as its explanation for showing these images:

> Only if all of us know the facts can we hope to prevent their repetition in the future.
>
> **British Movietone News, *22 April 1945***

All newsreels gave extensive coverage to the Belsen trials in the autumn of 1945.

Nevertheless, despite some initial reluctance to have the full details released, the British public did get a full understanding of what went on at Belsen within a week of its liberation and they were, of course, profoundly shocked. The war was over five-and-a-half years old in April 1945. Britain and its Empire had lost over four hundred thousand civilian and military casualties, virtually everything was rationed, including food, furniture, clothes, petrol and sweets and there were damaged and destroyed buildings in most of our major cities. Most people were utterly fed up with the war but, if they had ever wavered in their conviction that fighting the Nazis was the right thing to do, Belsen ended any such doubts. Attitudes towards the Germans visibly hardened after 19 April 1945. For British people, Belsen became the defining image of the Holocaust. Like the soldiers, the British people knew that they'd been in a just war.

Why Belsen was important

It is difficult to exaggerate the importance of Richard Dimbleby's report from Belsen. April 1945 was the final full month of the European war. The Russians were closing in on Germany from the east and the Allies from the west. Thousands on both sides were still dying each day. The Third Reich was being eradicated from the pages of history. Not surprisingly, the newspapers tended to concentrate their reporting on the military campaigns at the end of the war. Another big story broke on 12 April with the death of the American President F. D. Roosevelt, putting further pressure on editors. That's not to say that they ignored Belsen or any of the other liberated camps but they did choose other war stories for their main headlines. The most respected, but probably least read, of British newspapers *The Times* mentioned the liberation of Buchenwald on 16 April, but nothing from Belsen until 19 April, four days after British troops arrived there. Some fairly unsettling photographs of Buchenwald and a forced labour camp which the

US Army liberated appeared in the same edition, but nothing as graphic as the images which later surfaced.

The popular *Daily Mail* reported on the truce which enabled British troops to enter Belsen in its 14 April issue and then, beneath the headline "The Most Terrible Story of the War", began to give details of the liberation of the camp on 19 April. Two days later they published another story: "Belsen—The Final Horror". The *Daily Express,* probably the best selling newspaper in Britain at the time, captured the anger of the liberation when they commented on the Germans working to clear the site:

> These Germans must not pause in the hot wind. Never before, nor ever again, will they see Englishmen so angry as are the cool, grim, young men . . . left behind the fighting to see they do this task.
>
> **Daily Express,** *21 April 1945*

In North East England, where so many of the DLI troops lived, the *Evening Chronicle* in Newcastle did mention Belsen on 16 April but it was down to another paper from that city, the *Newcastle Journal and North Mail,* to publish a major article on 18 April. There was very strong competition for newspaper space and the monumental events of the closing stages of the European war took priority over the liberation of the camps in the papers whose size was limited due to wartime restrictions on the availability of newsprint. This left it up to Dimbleby to raise national awareness of this dreadful story. It is worth listening to him, as he battles with disbelief, carrying out his responsibilities as a witness. Tuning in to the BBC Home Service was something that people in Britain did on a regular basis throughout the war. After hearing this broadcast, the nation united in condemnation of the Nazi atrocities. Kramer quickly became known as "the Beast of Belsen", an insulting nickname used after the war, to other criminals for years to come. Dimbleby's broadcast, the later photographs and films and the newspaper coverage meant that the horrors of the camps would not be lost amongst the reports of the military campaigns in the final months of the war.

It is also worth remembering that, at the first Belsen trial in the autumn of 1945 (one of a whole series of war crimes trials), the world had the first real indication of what had happened at Auschwitz and this further hardened attitudes towards the Nazis. During the war, Churchill, Stalin and Roosevelt had indicated that they intended to prosecute the Nazis for war crimes. Belsen demonstrated that they had every intention of following up this promise.

Some historians have tried to play down the importance of Belsen, reminding us that the number of deaths was much smaller than Auschwitz (one million), Treblinka (eight hundred and seventy thousand), Belzec (six hundred thousand), Majdanek (three hundred and sixty thousand) and Sobibor (two hundred and fifty thousand). Similarly, we have been reminded that gas chambers didn't exist at Belsen and that, until the camp became horribly overcrowded in the early winter of 1944, conditions were better than at many other camps. That may be, but conditions in all of the camps were terrible and nowhere were they acceptable places of detention for millions of people who had not committed any crimes and were only imprisoned for reasons of race, sexual orientation or politics.

Of course, the number of those murdered at Belsen was very small in comparison to elsewhere but the total of those allowed to die was huge. Some who died of disease and starvation were burned in the crematoria, as were some of those who were murdered. Richard Dimbleby said, after visiting the crematorium:

They murdered ten thousand people in this fire in reprisal
for the murder of two SS guards.

Richard Dimbleby, BBC Home Service, April 1945
(IWM Sound Archives, recording no. 17714)

Kramer's pathetic defence at his trial, that air raids had made food
deliveries difficult, had been revealed quite soon after the liberation
to be a tissue of lies when the British troops visited the lavishly
stocked SS quarters and the Wehrmacht barracks. Kramer had
no chance of a reprieve, however, since it was known that he was
responsible for thousands of murders at Auschwitz.

Others trying to play down the significance of Belsen have pointed
to survivors' testimonies, which some claimed were exaggerated.
Whether this was the case or not, the cameras which took much
still and cine film of this camp of horror, coupled with the words of
Richard Dimbleby, did not lie. Belsen revealed Nazi Germany for what
it was: a barbaric regime that treated human life cheaply. The British
soldiers who first saw it were ordinary "Tommies" who had fought the
enemy courageously for six years. Many of them were from North East
England. Later, when the full horror of Nazi war crimes was revealed
and the horrendous number of deaths in the Polish extermination
camps became known, the tragedy of Belsen took its place in the final
reckoning of the Holocaust. But the moving and still picture images,
accompanied by recordings of eyewitness accounts provided the
world with the first evidence of Nazi barbarity. This news from Belsen
gave added impetus to the final push against Germany, hardened the
resolve of those determined to prosecute war criminals and reminded
the world that the Second World War was a righteous war that most
definitely had to be fought. *That* was the importance of Belsen.

Remember.

Members of the Durham Light Infantry
who have won the Victoria Cross

- John Byrne
- Thomas de Courcey Hamilton
- John Murray
- Thomas Kenny
- Roland Bradford
- Michael Wilson Heaviside
- Frederick Youens
- Arthur Moore Lascelles
- Thomas Young
- Richard Annand
- Adam Wakenshaw

ACKNOWLEDGEMENTS

I am most grateful to the following organisations and individuals:

- **Brian Cooper:** For his tireless proofreading. Any errors that remain are mine.
- **Kevin Sheehan:** For producing such exquisite maps specially for this book. His work is available from <http://www.manuscriptmaps.com>.
- **Imperial War Museum:** For permission to quote from sound recordings and reproduce photographs, and for a private screening of *German Concentration Camps Factual Survey.*
- **Trustees of the former DLI and Durham County Record Office:** For permission to reproduce the quotation from *The Story of Belsen* by Andrew Pares.
- **Lower Saxony Memorials Foundation:** For supplying images and granting permission for their use. Their website is at <http://bergen-belsen.stiftung-ng.de>.
- **London Evening Standard:** For permission to quote from the interview with Lilly Ebert, published on 26 January 2010.
- **Haymarket Books:** For permission to quote from *Diary of Bergen-Belsen 1944–1945* by Hanna Lévy-Hass (Haymarket Books, 2015).
- **The O'Brien Press:** For permission to quote from *I was a Boy in Belsen* by Tomi Reichental (2011).
- **BBC:** For permission to reproduce extracts from Richard Dimbleby's war report. The full recording can be heard at <http://www.bbc.co.uk/archive/holocaust/5115.shtml>.

BOOKS TO READ

About Belsen

Ben Shepherd, *After Daybreak: The Liberation of Belsen, 1945* (Pimlico, 2006).

Ian Baxter, *Belsen and its Liberation* (Pen & Sword Military, 2014).

Hanna Lévy-Hass, *Diary of Bergen-Belsen 1944–1945* (Haymarket Books, 2015).

Tomi Reichental with Nicola Pierce, *I was a Boy in Belsen* (O'Brien Press, 2011).

John Sadler, *Dunkirk to Belsen* (JR Books, 2010).

Andrew Pares, *The Story of Belsen* (pamphlet; Durham County Record Office).

About the Third Reich

Richard J. Evans, *The Coming of the Third Reich: How the Nazis Destroyed Democracy and Seized Power in Germany* (Penguin, 2004).

Richard J. Evans, *The Third Reich in Power: How the Nazis Won Over the Hearts and Minds of a Nation* (Penguin, 2006).

Richard J. Evans, *The Third Reich at War: How the Nazis Led Germany from Conquest to Disaster* (Penguin, 2009).

Richard Overy, *The Third Reich: A Chronicle* (Quercus, 2011).

Michael Burleigh, *The Third Reich: A New History* (Macmillan, 2000).

William L Shirer, *The Rise and Fall of the Third Reich* (Secker & Warburg, 1960).

About the Durham Light Infantry

William Moore, *The Durham Light Infantry* (Leo Cooper, 1975)

S. G. P. Ward and Nigel Poett, *Faithful: The Story of the Durham Light Infantry* (Thomas Nelson & Sons, 1962).

David Rissik, *The DLI at War: The History of the Durham Light Infantry 1939–1945* (Naval & Military Press, 2004).

Durham Light Infantry Museum, *Image of the Soldier: A Photographic History of the Durham Light Infantry from Crimean War to the Final Parade* (County Durham Books, 2005).

Memoir

Anne Frank, *The Diary of a Young Girl* (Puffin, 2007; first published in 1947).

Social History

Roy Hattersley, *Borrowed Time: The Story of Britain Between the Wars* (Little, Brown, 2007).
Juliet Gardiner, *The Thirties: An Intimate History* (Harper Press 2010).

The Origins of the Wars

Christopher Clark, *The Sleepwalkers: How Europe Went to War in 1914* (Penguin 2012).
Max Hastings, *Catastrophe: Europe Goes to War 1914* (William Collins, 2013).
A. J. P. Taylor, *The Origins of the Second World War* (Hamish Hamilton, 1961).
David Lowther, *The Blue Pencil* (Sacristy Press, 2012).

Military History

Antony Beevor, *D-Day: The Battle for Normandy* (Viking, 2009).
Ben Macintyre, *Double Cross: The True Story of The D-Day Spies* (Bloomsbury, 2012).

FILMS TO WATCH

The Longest Day (1962; D-Day).

Saving Private Ryan (1998; Normandy campaign).

Night Will Fall (2014; the Holocaust).

German Concentration Camps Factual Survey (2014).

Double Cross: The True Story of the D-Day Spies (2012).

Schindler's List (1993; the Holocaust).

Au Revoir Les Enfants (1987; the Holocaust).

The Diary of Anne Frank (films 1959, 1980; TV miniseries, first broadcast on BBC One, 2009).

Anne Frank: The Whole Story (TV miniseries, first broadcast on ABC, 2001).

PLACES TO VISIT

The Imperial War Museum, London

The Churchill War Rooms, London

The Imperial War Museum, Duxford

The Imperial War Museum North, Manchester

The DLI Museum and Art Gallery, Durham

The Bergen-Belsen Memorial, Lohheide, Germany

QUESTIONS FOR STUDENTS OF THE HOLOCAUST

1. Were the reasonably fit prisoners at the liberation of Belsen right to murder the kapos?
2. The ill-treatment and summary execution of SS guards at Belsen and elsewhere by Allied soldiers were war crimes. Should they have been prosecuted alongside the Nazis?
3. How would a nineteen-year-old soldier have felt on first arriving at Belsen? Put yourself in his shoes.
4. Give THREE reasons for the establishment of the Polish extermination camps.
5. Should SS guards have been punished for following orders, even if these orders including killing prisoners?
6. Why did so many convicted war criminals have their prison sentences shortened?
7. Why did film of the liberation of Belsen and other camps disappear by 1947?
8. What reawakened the world's interest in the Holocaust?
9. Should the authorities continue to pursue war criminals today, even though most are in their late eighties and nineties?

Lightning Source UK Ltd.
Milton Keynes UK
UKOW06f1713220316

270689UK00005B/321/P